HEART
OF A HAWK

DEBORAH H. TAINSH

Deborah H. Tainsh

To Bob —
Thank you for supporting
TAPS. May God bless.
your & your family's Continued
Journey. Sincerely Deb &
USMC Sgt Maj
DL Tainsh

Elva Resa * Saint Paul

Heart of a Hawk: One family's sacrifice and journey toward healing
©2006 Deborah H. Tainsh

Library of Congress Cataloging-in-Publication Data

Tainsh, Deborah H., 1954-
   Heart of a hawk: one family's sacrifice and journey toward healing /
Deborah H. Tainsh.
      p. cm.
   ISBN-13: 978-0-9657483-8-4 (pbk.)
   ISBN-10: 0-9657483-8-3 (pbk.)
   1. Iraq War, 2003—Personal narratives, American. 2. Iraq War, 2003—
Psychological aspects. 3. Tainsh, Patrick. 4. Soldiers—United States—
Correspondence. I. Title.
   DS79.76.T345 2006
   956.7044092—dc22
                        2006006703

Cover photo: Patrick Tainsh, photographer unknown. It was the only picture
ever taken on the digital camera Patrick's parents sent to him the Christmas
before he died.
Back cover photo: Tainsh family by Luther B. Benton, Jr., CW-4 USA Ret.

Design by Joel Tarbox and Andermax Studios. Set in Trajan Pro, Minion Pro.
Printed in United States of America.
1 2 3 4 5 6 7 8 9 10

A portion of the proceeds from this book is donated to
Tragedy Assistance Program for Survivors (TAPS) http://www.taps.org

Elva Resa Publishing http://www.elvaresa.com

For my husband, David, the Great Oak

In memory of your son and hero
Sergeant Patrick Shannon Tainsh
8-25-70 — 2-11-04

He is never dead, as long as Someone calls his name

~ AUTHOR'S NOTE ~

THERE ARE MANY STORIES about the lives of soldiers, the wars they fight on foreign soil, and the personal battles they fight afterward. But little is written about the heroes left at home, those who must smile bravely when they hug or kiss for the last time a loved one deployed to a war thousands of miles away.

These heroes—wives, husbands, children, brothers, sisters, mothers, and fathers—wake up every morning with a prayer on their lips, say several more during the day, and fall to sleep at night saying another. They either watch too much news or try to ignore it altogether. They look for a certain e-mail every morning, wait for the mail carrier, and hope the next ring of the phone is that call they've waited on for weeks. They write letters every day and mail a package once a week. They stand stoic and smile gratefully when someone asks how things are going and lets them know they pray for them and their loved ones.

Then, for some, the day comes they once believed happened only to others. The day a military chaplain and a casualty notification officer knock nervously on their door and deliver the worst conceivable message. These heroes are left with only a folded flag, a cabinet of awards and medals, a last letter, and a bittersweet pride that only military families understand.

It is because these stories often go unheard that after the death of my stepson, Sergeant Patrick Tainsh, on February 11, 2004 in Baghdad, I chronicled our family's life, sacrifice, and journey toward healing. The writing began as a catharsis, to sift through the many threads and knots that had formed the tapestry of my family's life. It was an attempt to make sense of—or at least understand—a part of it. I needed to see the replay of our family's life from Patrick's rebellious childhood to the day he said, "I want to do something that makes a difference," which led him to join the U.S. Army in 2000. I needed to ask God why our prayers weren't answered. I needed to pour my husband's and my anger, grief, and cry for understanding onto paper. And the story unfolded, telling the life of a son who sailed beyond his family's and best friend's expectations, met the call by his nation's commander in chief to enter Operation Iraqi Freedom, and subsequently left behind a memorable story that includes the anger, pain, and healing of those who loved him most, and the blessings brought to their lives by the many earthly angels who traveled with them through their journey of loss, grief, and search for healing.

Through this journey, my family's greatest learned truth is that no man, woman, or family is an island. We all need one another. And we must tell our stories to remember, to heal, and to immortalize those loved ones whose physical form was removed from our sight, but whose spirit always remains close, if only we stop and pay attention. We must remember the heroism of those left behind and be there for others who follow with loss.

As you enter this story you should know that some names have been fictionalized for privacy of others. However, the people, their words, and emotions are very real. I know because we clung to one another, shared with one another, and even read the minds of one another through the good and the bad. Although every person could not be mentioned, I did choose to use one fictional name, Rose, to represent all who gave so much love and support. I believe you all know who you are and what you mean to our family and to Patrick.

I pray this journey touches your heart and lets you realize how we are all an integral part of each other's lives and that hope will remain always strong within your hearts.

—*Deborah Tainsh*

"Hast thou not known? Hast thou not heard, that the everlasting God, the Lord, the Creator of the ends of the earth, fainteth not, neither is he weary? There is no searching of his understanding. He giveth power to the faint; and to them that have no might he increaseth strength."

—*Isaiah 40:28-29*

~ ONE ~

IT WAS THE FIRST DAY of spring, 2004, with the southern air settling at seventy-two degrees. The sky hovered above the house on Rocky Shoals Drive like a vaulted canopy of pale blue silk. David Tainsh sat at the breakfast table by the bay window. He read over again, one at a time, the letters his son had sent home almost a year ago. The one he held had been written like all the others: in small, quickly printed words, not always spelled or punctuated correctly, sometimes with two dates on one page, part in black ink, and part in red.

> *It's Apr 14, 03, 0655. I just got done cleaning weapon and hygiene. I'm still at an Iraqi military compound that we assaulted and seized. The Col said it's his now. I can tell you we are really close to Baghdad. We are still by ourself doing recon by fire missions and seizing weapons. We have had some really big finds and still no casualties. We are told the Suni and Shiites are fighting for territory but militia still thinks they can fight us.*
>
> *Apr 15. Today is a down day. Had to cut you off yesterday. I just got done doing laundry and taking a shower. We have 5 gal sun showers on our truck that me and the LT brought and now we are the most popular people here. I talked to Kacee today and told her to call you. I hope she did. Today USA Today interviewed a couple of people. They informed us that the war is pretty much over. But they aren't clearing routes. A lot of people are ready to go home. They can't wait to eat pizza or have a DR Pepper. It doesn't matter to me. Nothing matters except to do my job and bring my guys and myself home. Not for pizza and D.P. but for*

sanctuary. This country is so dirty. Trash is everywhere. There are so many wild dogs with disease. If they come into the camp we have to shoot them. How could a leader let his country turn into something like this? I just don't understand. Maybe I'm not supposed to understand. Around the Euphrates river it's like Heaven. Lush jungle, fruit trees, gardens and the bluest water you can imagine. Well I gotta go. Tell everybody Hi and I'm thinking about them.
Love,
Patrick

With shaky hands, Dave carefully placed the letter behind a clear sheet in the scrapbook, took another drink of coffee, and checked the time on the stove clock. It was nine-thirty. He would let his wife continue sleeping.

Sighing, he pushed back from the table, ready for a cigarette. He never smoked inside the house. If he could not quit, at least he could respect Deborah's request to smoke outside.

Exhaling smoke rings, he watched two squirrels challenge one another at the feeder on the oak tree. Birds called to one another from surrounding trees. His wife would know what kind they were. Some days she sat for hours watching, listening, and writing about the nature she observed. On any other first day of spring, Dave would have been looking forward to the dogwoods blossoming. But that resurrection symbol held nothing special for him since his son's death the month before. This bright spring day might as well have been a dark, lifeless visit to hell. He felt trapped in a foxhole, pinned down by a relentless barrage of loss, doubt, and anger. How would he ever escape? Putting his life on the line with the Marines was one thing. Losing his son was something else entirely.

Taking the last drag from his cigarette, he turned and crushed the butt out in the ashtray on the table behind him. His hand brushed the cane rocker where Deborah always sat. In front of the rocker stood the walnut stained footstool that Patrick had made in wood shop eighteen years ago. He was fifteen when he proudly brought the piece home from school. They lived in California then, and Dave was stationed at Camp Pendleton. The modest piece of woodwork was not the same now, with scratches and drops of paint covering its dark surface. As he studied how things had changed, Dave wondered where the time had gone. How his boy had grown to a man and now was gone.

Down the hall, Deborah lay watching the sunlight stretch between the slats of the window blinds. After three days of rain, she welcomed the balm. Rain and clouds only enhanced the heavy aura that had enveloped her home since February 12th. She stared at the white cathedral ceiling, trying to clear the heaviness from her eyes. Another restless night had kept her moving about the house after midnight, channel surfing, and finally drifting to sleep again on the sofa. It seemed she had just fallen to sleep when Dave woke her enough to send her back to the bedroom.

She rolled from the center of the bed where she always ended up in Dave's absence. She rubbed her back. Stiffness always set in when she missed her regular exercise. On the way down the hall toward the kitchen she tried not to look at the front door. Every time she passed the foyer, the memory of standing next to Dave and facing the Army chaplain and casualty notification officer in predawn hours returned. Passing through the family room with a glance through the glass door, she saw Dave on the deck.

He turned when she said, "Good morning," from the doorway.

"Well, good afternoon," he smiled in his continued attempt at morning humor. Peering at his wife, he thought she was the most beautiful woman in the world, no matter how ratty her shoulder length auburn hair looked or how puffy her eyes might be. Time had not yet taken a toll on her face or body. But then she still exercised and ate right. Something he'd slipped away from after the Corps.

"It's not afternoon yet, it's only ten o'clock."

"Close enough. Where's my morning kiss?"

Deborah stepped out to Dave. He wrapped his arms around her waist and pecked her on the lips.

"I haven't had my coffee yet," she said, returning the kiss.

Dave squeezed his wife once more and smiled. Since that knock on the door and the casualty notification officer's message of death, Deborah had been his saving grace. In past years he had taken her strength and endurance for granted and paid no attention to warning signs when she became distant. When he was stressed, stretched like an overextended rubber band, he could be hard with words, but he did all he could to let her know how much he loved her. He was doing the best he could now. He didn't want to lose her again like he had five years ago when she left him in California and returned to Georgia.

Deborah kissed him again and gently removed his arms from around her waist.

"Okay, get your coffee," he said, as she walked away.

Her cup from Snow Valley sat next to the coffeepot where he placed it every morning. She didn't talk much this early. She poured the cup of coffee, added two sugars and half-and-half, and returned to her rocking chair and footstool, as he knew she would. There she'd sit for nearly an hour in her own world of contemplation.

Dave returned to the breakfast table. Sealing a couple more letters inside the book, he thought back to last March when Patrick came home. He, Deborah, Patrick, and Jason, his stepson, had sat at this table and enjoyed their last Friday night dinner together. He supposed the memories would always play over and over like a needle stuck in a forty-five record.

Clutching the last letter, Dave sighed and read it again before placing it behind the plastic and closing the scrapbook. He rubbed his hand across the record of his son's last year then left the table and walked to the garage. He didn't like for Deborah to see him get emotional. From the open garage door he noticed the trees' tiny leaves emerging from the dark of winter, pushing their way toward sunlight. Dave thought how new life formed, how every year a single old oak or maple lost its brilliance down to the bone, then recreated it the next season. A beautiful process until the tree fell over from age or someone axed it down. He saw himself axed down, no longer owning the reproductive privilege. It wasn't fair. His only creation was gone. And there was no creating another.

Looking around the yard at last year's dead pine straw, he thought about a trip to Home Depot to fill in the spaces that needed color. At least he could dig some holes and fill them again to stop thinking of Patrick. Maybe. With another drag from his filtered Marlboro, he drifted to the one time a week when Patrick called home, always upbeat, always saying, "Don't worry, I'm doing good," or "Dad, don't believe everything you're hearing on the news." But that would never happen again. Shaking his head, Dave threw away another spent cigarette and turned toward the kitchen for his truck keys.

On the deck, Deborah sat in her rocker, the old friend who welcomed her every morning. With her toes on the edge of the footstool, she rocked gently back and forth. After waving Dave off to town, she returned to sipping coffee and soaking in the faultless nature. Brittle squirrels' nests rested on oak and maple limbs, new leaves barely visible, and in the sweet gum tree a finch's yellow head jerked with mechanical motions. Out of sight, crows and cardinals ministered to anyone who would listen. She studied the dogwood's scattered buds still hiding the white blossoms. As a child, her grandmother had told her the stained tips were symbols of Christ's nail-scarred hands.

"If you're really there, help us through this," she prayed. "I know you have the reason, but we're angry and hurting. We wanted Patrick back."

Staring at the chair next to the potted palm, she could still see her stepson. It was the morning of his thirty-second birthday, nineteen months ago. Seven months before Iraq. His dog tags hung against his bare chest, a cigarette dangling between his lips. He tore gift wrap from a book by Colonel David Hackworth and another by Tom Clancy. Patrick had always enjoyed reading. On top of his years of reading surfing, snowboarding, and skateboarding magazines, Patrick read about the military and airplanes. This was not unexpected. His dad was a career Marine, and Patrick had been born at Portsmouth Naval Hospital. From the time he was a boy, he had watched planes take off and land at Oceana Naval Air Station near Norfolk, and from age thirteen he had been around the big guns at Camp Pendleton in California. But he said he would never follow his dad's career. Not that he ever spoke of any careers except surfing or snowboarding. His joining the Army in 2000 had been a complete surprise to those who knew him.

Deborah peered at the footstool beneath her feet. Patrick had cut the pieces to fit the way he wanted: a rectangular top with scalloped edges and a hole in the middle. In the middle of each side support was a heart-shaped opening. Like his woodwork, Patrick's life had held a unique design with a strong heart. It had contrived and defied one event after another, giving Dave and her plenty of reasons to worry from the time he was thirteen. And it had worsened after his mother's death from cancer when he was seventeen. But the miracle was that four years ago, at age twenty-nine, he had turned his defiant heart over to the U.S. Army. Quite an irony since Patrick never cared for rules and regulations. His quantum leap from rebellious adolescence and young adulthood to a military career had kept everyone wondering if he would stick to it.

"I want to do something that makes a difference," he had told his best friend, Chris, who disbelieved until seeing Patrick in uniform after boot camp. Deborah had been surprised, too.

She joked with her stepson after hearing the news.

"All the way from dread locks and earrings to a crew cut and uniforms, not even a surf board hidden in the attic."

"I've slacked enough," Patrick said, grinning.

"Well I think you're a walking story just waiting to be written," she teased.

Patrick only laughed, saying, "I doubt that."

But he disproved all the cynics.

Deborah leaned her head against the back of the chair and closed her eyes. The fingers of a gentle breeze tapped against the wind chimes hanging from the porch cover. "I know you're out there, Patrick. We miss you. This is killing your dad. You gotta help me here."

She recalled the morning of the memorial service, twenty-eight days before. That morning, while standing on the porch sipping coffee and crisp air, she had noticed a red-tail hawk sitting on a branch of the oak, not fifty feet away. They stared at one another until Deborah turned to leave, filled with the memory of the spirit hawk legend, a myth of a great hawk with healing powers that made its way from Alaska to the eastern United States searching for "the one." Reaching a grassland village, the hawk found a small boy who had not spoken or smiled since his mother's death. When the young boy met the eyes of the great hawk, they knew they belonged to one another. The hawk extended its wings as the boy extended his arms, and just as it seemed the bird would collide with the child, there was a great flash of light and the hawk screeched a final time. The light faded and the hawk was gone. But the boy stood facing the sunlight, tears streaming down his cheeks, smiling as no one had ever seen.

To Deborah, a hawk's appearance at their oak tree seemed to say that over thirty-three years, Patrick had grasped his spirit hawk with all his soul, especially during his last four years of life. He had glowed and excelled because of it. Deborah opened her eyes and looked at the oak tree still waiting to release its leaves from its folded fists. Its wood had been the strength of the 1812 warship called Old Ironsides. Cannon balls had not been able to penetrate its solid layers. Deborah knew her husband, too, was built of impenetrable walls that could shut her out. Especially where Patrick was concerned.

~

Excluding their years of separation, Deborah and Dave had been married for almost twenty years. The moment that sealed their life together came on a Saturday in June 1983. They were introduced in Pine Hill, Georgia, at Jason's little league baseball game. Deborah was keeping the team's scorebook when an acquaintance, whose son was also playing, introduced the tanned, sinewy, balding Marine. A quick "hi" was all she said. That evening they crossed paths again at the pizza restaurant with another "hi."

On Sunday, Deborah walked along the shoreline at Beach Lake. Her friend Katrina waved and called to her from a blanket on the grass above the sand. Deborah waved back and strolled in her direction. Sitting next to Katrina was Dave, the man she had met the day before. He was staying with Katrina and her husband while closing the sale of his recently deceased mother's home in Columbus, Georgia, where he had been born but rarely returned.

Deborah and Dave's courtship consisted of seeing one another almost every day for two weeks. During that time, Deborah met Patrick, and Patrick and Dave met Jason. By the end of August Dave presented Deborah with an engagement ring and persuaded her to move to California, where they married in December.

Before their marriage, Dave had made no secret about his expectation to gain custody of his "wild pony" son who refused to be tethered. Patrick's mother had remarried, and her new husband could not handle Patrick's contemptuous mouth and independent behavior. Dave's mind was set when he learned that this man, once his best friend, had struck Patrick across the face. Two months after the wedding, Patrick arrived in California.

Deborah knew from experience the negativity that could be brought about with stepparents and children. She'd been raised by a stepfather from the time she was two and had taken a number of stripes from a leather belt for not moving fast enough when he spoke to her. But she believed she would make a good stepmom.

The night Patrick arrived at the apartment in California, thirteen years old and filled with anger, he was ready to fight his way all the way back to his mom's in Virginia Beach. He hated the move from a mostly undisciplined home life back east to across the country with his dad and a woman he barely knew.

Until that night, Deborah had been used to boys with haircuts above their ears, wearing jeans and t-shirts, usually carrying a baseball glove or a football. But Patrick entered her life with a surfboard under one arm and a skateboard under the other, sporting his bronze tan, bleached hair to his shoulders, and surfer shorts and a t-shirt in February. She didn't know then that his favorite movie character was Jeff Spicoli from *Fast Times at Ridgemont High*. In fact, she'd never heard of it until Patrick introduced her to the movie.

She had been appalled when Patrick responded to questions, especially from his dad, with a disrespectful-sounding "yeah" or "no" without "sir" or "ma'am" attached.

"It's not the way Patrick was brought up. Don't worry about it," was Dave's response when she wanted to discuss what she considered Patrick's disrespectful tone.

And with passing days, Patrick proved his grief with the world. Whenever the discipline reins felt too tight, he fought back with no care for consequences. His response to discipline was always the same, "Whatever," then he continued his own way.

One day when Patrick was fourteen, he had spent the day with buddies skateboarding instead of doing chores as asked. He became angry later that afternoon when he was told he couldn't go to a friend's sleepover. He slipped from the house and told a neighbor that his dad had beaten him, which he proved easily enough with the bruises he had acquired that day from crash and burns on skateboard ramps and concrete. While Deborah searched the neighborhood, Patrick sat inside a neighbor's house waiting for the police to pick him up. She discovered what happened from another neighbor only after Patrick was at the police station.

At the station, Deborah defended Dave and phoned the family psychologist she had convinced Dave to have Patrick see months before. The counselor spoke with the officer about Patrick's ability to gain attention, and they returned home with Patrick in tow. But none of it kept Dave from blaming her for the whole situation.

"It's your fault," he yelled. "If you hadn't told me to ground him, none of this would've happened."

They had the biggest fight of their early marriage that night, leaving Deborah in confused tears, Dave in a silent corner, and Patrick with no remorse, hoping the whole event would get him returned to his mother. And as time progressed with inevitable arguments, Deborah wondered if she were being punished because Jason, at his own request, had remained with his dad twenty-five hundred miles away in Georgia after she married Dave and the Marine Corps issued orders for California instead of Albany, Georgia, as Dave and she had hoped.

As months passed and Patrick still rebelled against rules as simple as making his bed or doing his school work, all Deborah heard was Dave's mantra, "Go to sleep. I have to work in the morning," when she wanted to talk after going to bed.

~

Sighing, Deborah threw the remaining coffee onto the grass. Behind the barren trees she could see the morning sun dancing on the lake. They had last fished there when Patrick was home a year ago. Being together as a family again had brought back happiness they had all missed for a number of years.

She thought back to something Dave had once said in the middle of an argument, that no one would come between him and his son, or before his son. But now, something *had* come between Dave and Patrick, and Dave was consumed with anger.

"God let me down," he had said. "Don't talk to me about God or faith. He didn't answer my prayers."

Deborah knew that sooner or later her husband would explode because he dwelled in silent anger and grief. She knew she had to handle her husband and herself better than she had in years past. She had to be his strength. She must not cave to the blast that had hit them. They both needed the spirit hawk, the prophetic bird of healing powers, to help move them beyond their loss. To help them see beyond the abyss that now held them captive.

But it seemed that happiness for Dave and her was an elusive dream. It came at short intervals before another battle.

They had repaired many dents and breaks. With time, they had managed to overcome obstacles. But this event had the power to place another iron curtain between her and her husband. Dave loved his son deeply, though to Deborah his love gripped those closest to him like tentacles, his way of making up for never knowing his own father and being raised a foster child. Losing what was most precious to him was like severing the tentacles and draining every ounce of life. Patrick had been his only line to the future and now he was gone. Deborah hoped she had learned enough about her husband to walk wisely on the path of coming days. She had spent hours weaving back and forth through the past twenty years of their life, Patrick's life, examining their family beginnings, how far they had come, and where they would go.

Deborah went to the kitchen. She placed two pieces of bread in the toaster and poured another cup of coffee. She wondered how many months or years it would take to shed the heavy cloud that enveloped her and Dave. This wasn't supposed to have happened to them. Tragedies happened to others. Though she had told herself at times over the past eleven months that *it could happen,* she hadn't truly believed it would.

We don't deserve another cataclysmic event in our lives, she thought. *Haven't we gone through enough over the years? Don't we deserve to have a complete family settled and happy?*

They had just pulled their marriage back together after being separated, and Patrick was on a remarkable path. But why should her family be any more fortunate than another? She shook her head to herself as she pulled the two slices of bread from the toaster and spread grape jam over them. Tears rolled down her face.

God, I'm trying to accept your will, but this is so difficult. You brought Dave and me back together. We're near Jason. You provided this beautiful home. Patrick was on a good path. All we were given was one year together before Patrick left for Iraq. Why, why, why?

Deborah took her coffee and toast to the family room and sat down on the sofa. A photo of Patrick and Dave stared at her from the top of the television. Dave's arm hung around his son's shoulders and Patrick's arm encircled his dad's waist. Both of them beamed with matching smiles. It had taken them years to become so close.

She placed the cup and plate on the coffee table and pulled a tissue from the box while remembering the day the picture was taken in front of the house. It was Patrick's first visit to their new Georgia home after she and Dave reconciled.

~

Dave had sworn he would never return to the south to live. A year before Patrick joined the Army, Deborah decided, after sixteen years, that she and Dave had grown worlds apart, with nothing left to hold them together. Years of disagreeing and arguing had taken its toll. She wanted to return to Georgia and leave behind the static Southern California landscape with its postage stamp yards, where the neighbors' beige plaster always faced her. But most important, she wanted to live near Jason, who had tired of traveling every summer to California crowds and freeways. To Dave's astonishment, she moved without him. At the time, Patrick was living his own life, wandering from the California coast to the mountains of Nevada and a few other states, surviving as a cook.

After three years in Georgia, Deborah, who had never been one to live forever without trying to find resolutions, sent another letter to the home she and Dave owned in Oceanside.

> *Dear Dave,*
> *I don't know if you will receive and open this letter or not. And if you have someone new in your life, I am not sending this to cause problems. I am writing because I cannot live the rest of my life without resolution and forgiveness for all the harsh, angry words that we've said to one another in the past, and all the pain we've caused one another because we're both so strong willed and have such different ways of looking at living life. I was so naïve and immature when we married. But I had to grow up fast to deal with the new life we had in California. In this growth, I found I had to learn to be headstrong and willful to deal with your strong personality. I also had to learn independence since you were overseas and in the field so much.*

I know that my growing independence, going to college, and falling away from the old southern school of the woman's place caused issues as well. And once I learned to have opinions, we never seemed to agree on much of anything. We had battles that left issues to fall where they would. But beyond all of that, I have always loved you for the strong, but hardheaded man that you are, and admired you for bringing yourself from nothing to a successful career. I was always proud to be the wife of a U.S. Marine. I always felt safe. I was blessed that you didn't drink and carouse around. I always had a beautiful home, a great car, beautiful clothes, and all a woman could want. I just couldn't live with argumentative confrontations anymore and feeling as though our life together had come to a boring standstill on freeways, the sofa, and television. And the worry over Patrick's coming and going. But I feel that I did give some good dedicated years to being a supportive Marine Corps wife and stepmom during some very tough times.

I feel it's my time now without argument to choose being near my birth son and smelling the clean air of country living and not California smog. But know that you are special and I am special, too. We are just two very different personalities. I hope you can forgive me as I have forgiven you for things I know we both regret. I wish you all the happiness that you deserve.

Deb

A week after Deborah mailed the letter she received a response from Dave that left her feeling their life together was not over.

Deborah,
What a wonderful letter I found in the mailbox. No, there is no other person in my life, and never has been except for you. I have always loved you and always will. I've never given up hope on us. I know that all that has happened in our lives has been a combination of a lot of

things. We are all to blame, not just one of us. I hope you will call me or write again, but I don't want to push you into anything. You will always be my punkin. I have missed you so much. But I knew that you were adamant about my staying away from you once you left here. All in all it has probably been for the best. I know that my temper caused problems, and I have worked very hard on that. By the way, Patrick has joined the Army. You wouldn't believe how he has turned his life around. I think we are closer now than we have ever been. Oh, how I have prayed for you to come back to my life. I had given up. Finally realizing that I can't make you love me or be here. But I still prayed. I hope to hear from you again.

Love Always,
Me

Three months later, in spring 2002, with Patrick's and Jason's blessings, they had put their lives back together, on a happy upswing. But now, spring 2004, a war had cost them more than they could have ever comprehended.

~

Deborah stared at the photo of Patrick and Dave, telling herself that fulfilled dreams or tomorrows were never promised to anyone or any family. The trick was finding a place in silent moments where reconciliation with events could flow across the grieving like warm water spilling over cold, stiff fingers. Though sometimes, getting to the water took time.

Deborah knew that Dave and she could have grieved years ago when Patrick was spending his energy running with the wrong crowds and shuffling from one dead-end job to another. But for some reason, they had been spared the pain until now. From a human standpoint, the past months held inexplicable events, but Patrick had been at his best, felt his best, and given his best, without wanting as much as a thank you in return.

Hearing the garage door heave upward brought Deborah back to her now-cold toast. She hurried to the bathroom, threw off her clothes, and stepped into the shower. She didn't want Dave to see she had been bawling. She didn't want to do anything that intensified his anxiety. He hated to see her cry because he didn't know how to deal with it.

~

Deborah had cried more than she should have during their early years of marriage after receiving custody of Patrick. But there were good memories, too, such as the Mother's Day when Patrick kissed her on the cheek and handed her a vase of flowers with a card that said, "Thanks for all you do for me." She had saved it inside a photo album. And there was the frustrating, but humorous Christmas Day they attempted skiing together at Snow Valley when Patrick was fifteen. Though an excellent surfer and skate boarder, Patrick had thrown his skis down the hill after falling and walked the rest of the way to the bottom of the mountain. He chose snowboarding after that, learning to hang ten down a mountain of snow as well as he did on a wave. And there were the hugs he gave for buying his favorite Vans sneakers or surf brand clothes.

But after three years in California, Dave received orders for Japan, and Deborah worried about handling Patrick alone. Her stepson saw an opportunity to take the situation into his own hands. Without a word to anyone, to escape any tethering or arguments while his dad was away, he sold the car he had been given for his sixteenth birthday: a sixty-five Nova Dave paid to have painted candy apple red and upholstered with black leather "roll and tuck." Silver mag wheels set it off. After selling the car for enough to buy the airline ticket, Patrick flew to his grandmother's in North Carolina.

After locating Patrick, Dave finally acquiesced and let his son remain where he was. In spring, Dave returned from Okinawa; by winter, Patrick called to say his mother was hospitalized with cancer. Three weeks later she died. Patrick was seventeen. Deborah insisted Dave go to North Carolina to be with Patrick during the memorial and to bring him back home.

After his return to California, Deborah and Dave continued the struggles with Patrick's disinterest in completing school, his insatiable desire to surf and skateboard, and his refusal, unless there were heated arguments, to do his part around the house.

After his eighteenth birthday, Patrick told Deborah, "I don't want to live with your rules anymore."

All Deborah could say was, "Well, you can move anytime you like. We're no longer legally responsible for you." After that, Patrick had taken complete charge of his own destiny, which led him down an eleven-year road of instability, and then uphill, such a short time ago, to a promising career.

~

Deborah turned off the shower. She applied the towel as roughly to her skin as the analyzed past had been to her senses. Neither brought comfort.

"Hey, I'm home." Dave called from outside the bathroom. "I'll be out in the yard."

"I'll be done in a few," Deborah answered.

After stepping from the shower, she pulled on her robe and opened a vanity drawer where she kept socks. She removed a pair of thick-woven red and black ones with a tiny gold bell sewn on each ankle that Patrick had given her the last Christmas he was home. That Christmas had been more special for Dave and her than any they had experienced.

Pulling on the socks and thinking about that 2002 holiday season, she wondered if somewhere in her subconscious she had known there would never be another like it. In hindsight, she felt she had somehow foreseen that no future holidays would ever be the same as the New Year that saw her family together and happy, then opened its mouth like the Red Sea, restraining, temporarily, the walls of raging water that had waited to crash into their lives.

~ TWO ~

IN THEIR NEW HOME IN GEORGIA, 2002 brought the first holiday season that Deborah and Dave had shared with both their sons, simultaneously, in ten years. After Thanksgiving and Patrick's return to Fort Polk, Louisiana, Deborah dragged Dave to shop for the ten-foot artificial fir she wanted placed in the dining room in front of the arched windows.

"So, how about this one!"

"I'm happy if you're happy," Dave said to his wife. He loved to see her act like a little girl spilling over with excitement. After being separated, this promised to be their happiest holiday season ever. He was sure his bank account would be broken by the time Deborah finished Christmas shopping. But he didn't care, as long as she was smiling.

After transporting the huge box from the Hobby Lobby store to their house, he struggled to place all the branches in their slots and then stand the tree straight.

"Great job, hon," Deborah said, standing back with folded arms, admiring the tree. "I'll need your help getting the ribbon wrapped around and to the top."

"Don't I get a break?"

"Not till we're finished here!"

Deborah reached her hand toward Dave's to help him up from his seat on the floor. After thirty minutes, white lights, red silk poinsettias, and strands of wide gold ribbon covered the tree.

"Well, I gotta have a smoke," Dave said, after placing the final poinsettia on top of the tree. "Then I'll work on the yard."

Before dark, the new white wire deer with moveable heads and white lights sat on the hill at the top of the driveway, and three-foot-tall green and red electric candy canes stood attached to pine trees.

Inside the house with Bing Crosby crooning *White Christmas,* Deborah finished decorating with nutcrackers, garland, and candle arrangements. She hung stockings for Dave, Patrick, Jason, and herself from the mantle of the fireplace.

"It never fails to amaze me how you make a house look so good," Dave said after ambling through the family and dining rooms.

"Well, you guys always enjoyed Christmas toy lands," she said, "I'm certainly not disappointing you this year."

"And you're not," Dave said, kissing her. "I'm going to the store for cigarettes, do you need anything?"

"I don't think so. See you when you get back."

Deborah went to the kitchen and pulled a wine glass from the cabinet.

And I'm not disappointing myself, she thought, and smiled as she poured a glass of white zinfandel and returned to the dining room to admire the blinking lights. She was finally at home in Georgia with her husband and her son Jason, and Patrick was coming home from Fort Polk for a ten-day Christmas leave. Deborah was especially excited because Jason's girlfriend, Sindy, already an integral part of the family, would be there, and they would meet Patrick's girlfriend, Kacee Riaquez, for the first time. She and Dave had heard from Patrick in September that he had met someone special.

"She's smart and hot!" He told his dad over the phone.

At thirty-two and never married, their son had not entered a serious relationship since gaining a broken heart in his twenties. After a two-year relationship during his California surfer life, the girl had left him with no explanation.

"So, how did you meet this girl?" Dave asked as Deborah listened on the extension the night Patrick called to share his news.

"Out in town, coming out of Wal-Mart. She made a comment about my legs, so I went back to talk to her. She had a sense of humor and a great smile. She's in the Guard and teaches first grade. Plus she's got class," he said.

Deborah smiled to herself again and straightened a few of the poinsettias that set crooked in the tree branches. *It's going to be wonderful to have a house full of happy people,* she thought.

On Christmas Eve, Dave laughed and shook his head.

"Do you think you bought enough? I can hardly move in here." In the dining room, gifts covered the floor from the tree base to the table legs.

"Well, this year's special, you know that," Deborah said. "This is our first Christmas together after all this time. I can't wait for the kids to open all this stuff. You know they love being splurged on even if they are grown. Anyway, they need to enjoy this now. Once we have grandkids they won't get all the attention."

Dave grinned. "Yeah, I remember that Christmas when Patrick and Jason were teenagers. You bought those toy trucks and water guns along with new skateboards."

"I still have the pictures with their big grins and playing around. I might have to bring out the album for Sindy and Kacee to see."

"I'm sure they'll love that," Dave laughed and kissed his wife.

"Hey, what's up?" said Patrick, who had arrived the day before.

"Just Christmas. How was your run?" Dave grabbed his son around the shoulders.

"It was good. I made it to Flat Rock Park and back."

"Well, that's a good eight miles," Deborah said. "Sorry I couldn't make it with you."

Deborah's long distance running days had come to an end a while back due to an achy back and knees. "Jason and Sindy should be here by six for dinner and gift opening. I've got crab legs and shrimp cooling in the fridge."

"Sounds good, I'll get a shower."

Deborah watched her *bonus son,* a term she liked better than *stepson,* as he strolled from the dining room. "He looks so good. He really filled out," she said, reaching her hand toward Dave to help her from the floor where she'd just completed wrapping the final gifts.

After dinner, Patrick, Jason, and Sindy howled with laughter after tearing gift wrap from boxes containing remote controlled vehicles. Four-wheel-drive trucks with working headlights for Patrick and Jason, and a Mercedes for Sindy.

Having opened their matching Tommy Hilfiger shirts, Deborah said, "You've got to put these on so I can take a picture of all three of you."

With Sindy in the middle, they huddled together in front of the fireplace without an argument. After Deborah finished the photos, Patrick was ready to play.

"Well, let's try these remotes out," he said, as he picked up his red truck and headed toward the back door followed by Jason and Sindy. From inside the garage Deborah and Dave stood with their arms around one another and watched as though observing three small children laughing and maneuvering their toys up and down the driveway.

By noon on Christmas Day Patrick was in Atlanta to meet Kacee at her sister's house. She had flown there from Louisiana several days earlier.

"We hope you like lots of hugs," Deborah said later in the evening after Kacee entered the family room with Patrick.

Dave rose from his recliner. "Well, I can see why Patrick grabbed hold of you." Grinning, he wrapped his arms around the petite brunette and squeezed.

Kacee laughed with confidence. "Well, Patrick's told me so much about his family, I feel like I already know everybody."

"Well, consider yourself family this moment. Don't be shy. Make yourself at home."

"Yes sir. I will," Kacee replied.

"There is one rule," Dave said. "Don't call me sir. I'm not a sir."

Kacee laughed again. "Oh yeah, I forgot about that. Patrick told me not to do that. It'll be hard for me to remember. I'm a pure-bred ol' time southern girl."

"Don't pay him any attention, Kacee," Deborah smiled from her corner of the sofa near Dave. Reaching to hold his hand she said, "He's just a big teddy bear. Sindy has him wrapped around her finger. As of now, you've got him, too."

Deborah remembered hearing from Patrick that Kacee had lost her dad when she was ten and that her mother was in a nursing home with Alzheimer's. They hoped to help Kacee enjoy the holidays as much as they could.

"Have you talked to Jason yet?" Dave looked toward his son.

"Yeah, I talked to them earlier today. We're all going to a movie tonight after dinner and then to Jason's house for a while."

"Get your laugh hat on," Deborah told Kacee. "Getting those three together is a party by itself."

"I'm looking forward to it," Kacee smiled from where she and Patrick had taken a seat on the sofa.

"I know you just got here, but I'd like to go ahead and take a picture of the two of you next to the Christmas tree. Besides, I think Santa left something for you."

In the dining room Kacee sat in Patrick's lap, his chin on top of her head, while Deborah took one picture after another to welcome Kacee to the family. Then she handed Kacee the gifts.

"You guys didn't have to do this. This is so nice."

"We know," Dave said, as the three reentered the family room. "But everyone who visits the Tainsh home at Christmas must leave with something."

Deborah watched Kacee remove the candles and Victoria's Secret lotions from the gift bags while Patrick sat next to her, beaming.

After all the down years, it's a perfect Christmas, Deborah thought, smiling, complete with satisfaction. Dave turned on Fox News. The war in Afghanistan was in full force. Troops were being organized in Kuwait for an impending attack against Saddam Hussein in Iraq.

Deborah sighed, knowing Patrick's unit, the Second Armored Cavalry Regiment, was on standby for further orders.

"I'm not letting this squelch our holidays," Deborah said, kissing Dave, then asked him for Christmas night to turn off the television. "We've been too long overdue for this kind of happiness," she whispered. "Let's not spoil it tonight."

~ THREE ~

CLOUDS THAT LOOKED LIKE brush strokes covered blue sky on Friday, March 14th. Patrick was on the way home for the first time since the Christmas holidays, and the last time before deploying to Iraq.

Deborah put her arms around her husband as he stood in front of the back yard grill.

"Is that barbeque ready?"

"I think so, I'm taking it up now. I think two hours is plenty of simmering."

"Well, the baked beans, potato salad, and sweet tea are ready."

"Smells good out here." Patrick walked into view from the side of the house. He was wearing his knee-length surfer shorts and a t-shirt that hung over his waist. His hair was cut as short as the scalp allowed.

"Well, it's about time you got here. I thought you'd be here earlier. How ya doing, Bud?" Dave turned to embrace his son.

"I thought I heard a car," Deborah said, following behind her husband.

"Sorry. I left later than I thought I would. And I'm sure hungry."

"Jason's on the way. We'll chow down as soon as he gets here," Dave said. "By the way, I found the release on the Internet about the regiment preparing for Iraq. It said the Second Armored Cavalry Regiment is a major unit of the 18th Airborne Corps and has received orders to deploy."

"Yeah, that's us," Patrick said. "A regiment of more than four thousand."

While listening to Patrick, Dave moved the roast from the grill to a platter. The release was his and Deborah's new reality.

Not some new television show that could be re-acted, rewound, or moved fast forward if you didn't like the first take, but a reality with the taste of vinegar moving down their throats. When he showed the information to Deborah, her solemn comment was, "Well, I guess it's for real."

After taking a seat in one of the cane rockers and lighting a Marlboro, Patrick said, "We're supposed to be outta here by one April."

"Well, that's a few weeks away," Deborah said, not wanting to think beyond having her family together now. "Let's don't ruin dinner with any of this."

With the food on the table, Dave sat at the end of the pine table that he and Patrick had refinished together. He and Deborah laughed as Patrick and Jason poked fun at one another, calling each other by the nicknames they had assigned to each other years ago: Patricia and Jassica.

"Let's go to Benning and play some golf in the morning," Jason said, between shoveling in mouthfuls of food.

"Sounds good to me. I brought my golf clubs to leave in the storage room. What time you wanna go?"

"Well, depends on how late we stay up tonight." Jason chuckled and held up his Corona.

More serious, Jason looked at Patrick. "Hey man, you sure you're really gonna be headin' for Iraq?"

"That's the word if Saddam doesn't get out, which I doubt. We're waiting to see if we're gonna be able to go in through Turkey. Doesn't look like they're gonna let us, though."

"Well man, you just take care of yourself. Don't be playin' no hero business."

Patrick laughed. "Won't be no days like that, dude." He sounded as laid back as Jeff Spicoli from 1982. Dave remembered the days almost twenty years ago when Deborah thought she would pull her hair out because Patrick wanted to *be* Spicoli, not exactly a role model. Patrick's surfer vocabulary, *gnarly, rad, hey dude, let's party,* had been strengthened mimicking Sean Penn's California high school surfer character. A nice guy, but not exactly focused on education and status quo.

Dave laughed to himself remembering the boys' first summer together in California after Deborah and he married. Jason had flown there from Georgia. He was almost eleven and Patrick fourteen that summer of '84. Deborah returned from work every day livid about the calls she'd received.

"He's picking on me, Mama." Jason would say.

"No, he's picking on me," said Patrick, although at the time Patrick towered over Jason, who didn't reach his current height of six-two until twelfth grade, leaving Patrick behind at five-nine.

"He's putting my toothbrush in the toilet bowl, Mama."

"No, it's Jason. He's putting my hair brush in the toilet."

"Mama, we got kicked out of the movie theater. Pat was too loud."

"No it was Jason, he was the one."

Although Deborah had often lost patience, raised her voice to reprimand both boys, and complained to Dave, she did her best to do what was right. She treated the boys equally. And during Patrick's school year she was at his call for help with schoolwork, though with his disinterest in school and studying, Patrick concocted many a scheme that placed immeasurable pressure on the marriage.

Tonight, Dave watched his wife's face glow like a child among best friends. Looking at his son's matured, firm jaw, Dave listened to Patrick answer Jason's questions about his military life and college classes, now on hold until his deployment ended. He soaked in Deborah's smiling face. With the past behind them, their boys' laughter around the table created the moments they had always wanted. Though he had never believed happy memories would occur at a home in the same southern area where he was born, the place he swore he'd never return to after joining the Marines in '66. After his mother died in 1983, the year he and Deborah met, he had no living relatives in this place. During past years of their marriage, he'd been adamant in telling his wife that he had not left or lost anything in this part of the country, and he had no intention of retiring here.

What he had never taken into consideration was that Deborah had plenty of reason to return. Jason and her other family members lived here. Dave had ignored her feelings for years, and that had added to her reasons to leave him in California. But after three years apart, and a letter from the woman he adored, he gave in without another argument. Patrick had already joined the Army. With Fort Polk nearer to Georgia than Southern California, everything turned out for the best. It had to be a sign that they were meant to be here when their California home sold the day it went on the market, and the home they now sat in was purchased the day after. It was the home Deborah had always talked about, two acres of woodlands, eleven miles from town, perfect for their sons and future wives and grandchildren. He had fallen in love with the house, which sat in a small valley at the foot of a winding driveway. Birds trilling and squirrels scampering in the brush were the only apparent noises. Dave had finally confessed to Deborah that he was more calm and relaxed than he'd ever been in his entire life. And on Patrick's first visit home last August, the one-time surfer embraced the peaceful privacy along with the lake behind the house where they fished together. For anyone who believed in fate, it was apparent that Dave, Deborah, and their sons were meant to be together as a family.

"Okay, guys, let's give Mom a break and clean up the kitchen," Jason said, breaking into Dave's thoughts.

"Well, thank you. I won't turn down that down, although my honey usually gives me too many breaks anyway."

"Yeah, I'm your slave," Dave said, grinning.

"That was good stuff," Patrick said. "I guess it'll be a long time before I'm fed like that again."

"We'll ship you a frozen steak now and then," Jason laughed. "You can build a fire in the desert and throw it on."

"Yeah, man, along with taking a bath from my helmet."

"Okay, guys. I'm giving this up to you," Deborah said and went to the family room.

After the cleanup, Dave lounged with Deborah and the boys near the big screen television, channel surfing back and forth from basketball to news. Bush urged Saddam Hussein to go into exile or face war. Ever since the terrorists' attack on 9-11 that had sent hijacked airliners exploding against New York's Twin Towers and the Pentagon and crashing into a Pennsylvania field, the war against the Taliban and search for Bin Laden continued in Afghanistan. There were reports that Hussein had weapons of mass destruction that were an imminent threat to the United States. The sand was running from the hourglass for a halt or an advance into Baghdad, Iraq. Kuwait was the staging ground.

On Saturday evening, Dave was resting in his recliner watching a Gene Autry western when the back door opened.

"Hey, we're back! What's for dinner?"

Patrick and Jason walked in the kitchen and looked over Deborah's shoulder at the skillet.

"Smells good. We're starving," Patrick said.

"We're having chicken and shrimp fajitas. You guys might want to clean up."

"Sindy's on the way over," Jason said, grabbing a chicken strip from the pan.

Sindy was half Korean, all of five-foot-one and one hundred pounds. Her amusements included jumping on Jason's or Patrick's back and having them ride her around like a kid on a bronco.

Deborah thought about Kacee. She wished she were here, too. She turned toward Patrick who was pouring a glass of ice tea. "Have you talked to Kacee?"

"Yeah, I called and let her know I got here. She's so busy with school stuff and the Guard that she couldn't leave. You know her unit's on the list for Afghanistan."

Deborah remembered Kacee had mentioned her impending deployment the last time they spoke.

"Hey, how was your golf game?" Dave yelled from his recliner.

"Let's don't talk about it!" Both Patrick and Jason chimed as the back door opened. Sindy bounded into the kitchen, straight on to Patrick's back.

"Hey, Patricia! Are we ready to eat yet? I'm starving."

"You're always hungry," Jason said. "Get off that boy's back. Don't wear him out before he leaves the country. He'll have to carry a big enough pack when he gets to Iraq."

Sindy dropped to the floor and walked to Deborah.

Deborah smiled, accepting Sindy's arm around her waist and a kiss on the cheek before the petite cutie headed to the family room to tease Dave.

Stirring peppers and onions in the skillet, Deborah thought about how thankful she was that she and Dave had somehow survived the often nasty bumps of the past with her husband's sergeant-major mentality and once wild-child.

"Hey, Mom, we ready to eat yet?" Jason's voice vaporized Deborah's thoughts.

"I'm putting it on the table now." Deborah raked the chicken, shrimp, and vegetables into bowls and set them next to warm tortillas. "Come and get it," she called.

After dinner, Sindy and the boys went off, saying, "We'll see you later. Don't wait up." They were going to have their own bon voyage party for Patrick.

"I'm going to miss having the three of them together," Deborah said as they disappeared outside. That night, she lay awake waiting for the back door to open and close behind a grown son. Dave could only think about Sunday, the last day he would see his son for more than a year.

Following a late Sunday breakfast, Dave sat on the sofa with Patrick. Together they reviewed the documents deploying soldiers leave behind. The whole matter seemed surreal. Suddenly it was difficult to believe that Patrick, who had relinquished his surfboards and snowboards just three years earlier, was on the way to man a fifty-caliber weapon on top of a Humvee.

"After I get back to Polk I'll call you with storage information on the car," Patrick told his dad, then added, "but here's the power of attorney and beneficiary information," handing over the papers.

Dave had gone through the same exercise with Deborah in 1990 when he prepared for the Persian Gulf. But this time it wasn't

Dave leaving, telling his wife not to cry, that everything would be fine. This was a different story.

This time his only child was leaving to face Iraq's Republican Guard and insurgents. This time, Dave carried the same weight as Deborah, if not more.

On Sunday evening, Dave and Deborah hugged their thirty-two-year old son. Dave took final hold of Patrick's shoulders and looked straight into his eyes with parting words.

"We love you, son. Don't ever forget that. Be careful, keep your head down, and don't trust anybody." Dave held no doubts about realities that loomed over his son's coming year. His time in Vietnam had included Dong Ha and Con Tien during the Tet Offensive. He remembered facing an enemy head on, some no more than children who would throw a grenade or point a rifle in your face. The time would come to make crucial decisions. Kill or be killed. With silent prayers, Dave held his wife around the shoulders as they watched their son's car disappear, the taillights fading in the darkness. They knew the next word from him would be by phone, telling them he was boarding a plane for Iraq.

~ FOUR ~

DEBORAH SAT IN A BOOTH across from her husband at their favorite restaurant. Old washboards hung from the tin ceiling along with an antiquated mule harness. Aged, yellowed newspapers and heirloom family black and whites hung on the four walls.

In the booth in front of them, wearing green fatigues and high and tight haircuts, sat three soldiers from Fort Benning, a base that was ten miles away.

"I'm going to get their tab," Dave said quietly. Deborah agreed.

When the waitress approached the table, Dave asked her to bring him the soldiers' bill and to please keep it anonymous. He and Deborah later overheard one of the young men tell the waitress to tell whoever it was, thank you. Then they heard the soldiers talking, wondering who at the multiple tables had paid their tab.

"Hey, you two. How are you?"

Rose Hendrix stood next to the booth. She was an old friend, a foster sister from Dave's childhood. They had become reacquainted six months ago, after Rose approached Dave at a local restaurant because he looked familiar.

"We're doing good. How 'bout yourself?" Dave said, as he stood and offered Rose a hug.

"Doing as well as can be expected. I stay busy with my job at the school, look after Daddy, and keep in touch with my kids." Rose, widowed while her son and daughter were just children, had never remarried. "How's Patrick doing? The last time I saw you he was on the list for Iraq."

"His unit's still on standby. We're just waiting for the call," Dave told her.

"Well, my son's unit is on the list, too. I guess we can all keep prayer vigils together."

"We'll keep your family in our thoughts," Deborah said. "Let us know if you need us for anything."

"Same here," Rose said, then dismissed herself to join a friend waiting at a table on the other side of the room.

That night, thunder and lightening played in the background of an easy rain. Deborah wrote *Pat called* on the calendar's date of March 19th. His unit, still on notice, was locked down at Fort Polk. She pulled her sweater from the back of a kitchen chair and wrapped it around her shoulders. Picking up a book of poetry, she went to the family room where she lay down on the sofa and propped her feet in Dave's lap. Fox News repeated updates on the banner moving across the bottom of the television screen as Bill O'Reilly tossed out the "most ridiculous items of the day." At 9:45 p.m. *Hannity and Colmes* was interrupted. The United States terror alert was coded high. In Baghdad it was 5:45 a.m., and air raid sirens pealed through the air.

Dave removed his feet from the coffee table, placed them on the floor, and leaned forward with his elbows on his knees.

"Well, the war's on. I hope they hit Hussein's hideout," he said, as fighter pilots dropped smart bombs at strategic locations.

Deborah sat up and placed her book on the coffee table. She picked up the tan leather journal Dave had given her last Christmas. She wrote notes while bursts of light from bombs scattered across the television screen.

She would never forget the day bombing had launched the Persian Gulf War. Dave was the sergeant major then assigned to the Air Traffic Control Unit in Tustin, California, one of the first units deployed to air traffic control towers at Bahrain airport. Deborah swore she'd never watch news again after watching exploding tomahawk missiles in real time, night after night.

But here she was, twelve years later, waiting with the nation to hear the President's statement at 10:15 p.m. Eastern time. As dawn unfolded across Baghdad, birds flew in front of the camera lens and traffic lights blinked.

"They're brave," Deborah said. "I can't believe people and cars are moving on the Baghdad streets."

Daylight pierced the clouds hovering above a mosque as President Bush spoke: "The peace of a troubled country now lies in the hands of our men and women and a coalition of more than thirty-five countries. We come to Iraq with respect for its citizens. We will not live at the mercy of an outlaw regime. We will accept no outcome but victory."

"It's too much information," Deborah finally said, "to see America's soldiers fighting the enemy. It's like a twenty-first century coliseum."

Yet in days that followed she was constantly pulled to the television, just like Dave, while they waited for Patrick's departure.

On Wednesday, April 1st, Deborah picked up her car keys and walked outside wearing jeans and a baseball cap. Dave stood in the yard trying to decide if the grass needed fertilizer.

"Honey, I'm headed to Wal-Mart," she said to her husband from the garage door. "I shouldn't be gone long."

"Sure, I'll bet I'll see you in about four hours," he teased.

On the way up the driveway, Deborah stopped and yelled, "Hey, you," out the car window. When Dave turned she blew him a kiss. He smiled in return.

Twenty minutes later she meandered up and down Wal-Mart's aisles to pass the time. With mouthwash, deodorant, and razor blades in the basket, she drifted to the cashier's line where two teenage boys stood in front of her. She wondered if they were skipping school. She thought about Patrick, when he had been fifteen or sixteen with no cares in the world except how much arguing he could do to get out of trouble for not cleaning his room, bringing home failing grades, or skipping school to surf.

~

When Patrick was in ninth grade, Deborah received a call from one of his teachers who wanted to confirm that Deborah had signed a note for Patrick to leave school early for a doctor's appointment. The conversation led to the discovery that Patrick had forged her name on prior notes so he could ditch school. It was another day of learning how difficult being a stepmom could be.

"I've never signed any notes!" Deborah said frantically. "Don't release him. I'll call his dad." She didn't feel she had the right to take the matter into her own hands.

The situation only added to existing tension. Patrick had called Dave at work several weeks before, claiming to be sick. On that day, Dave had driven twenty miles from Camp Pendleton to the school, taken Patrick home, then gone back to work. After arriving home that day, Deborah found that her stepson had apparently entertained a young lady in the master bedroom. When Dave arrived, there was no Patrick, only a crying, frustrated, angry wife.

"I don't understand any of this!" Deborah yelled. "How and why would a fourteen-year-old do something like this? All the stuff he does. He lies, he skips school, and you know I've found cigarettes hidden beneath the toilet bowl cover."

Dave gritted his teeth.

"Where the hell is he now?"

"I haven't seen him since I got here," she cried as she stripped the linens from the bed. Dave picked up the empty Trojan package from the floor, threw it in the bathroom trash, and stormed from the apartment with the front door slamming behind him.

Years after such frustrating events, Deborah and Dave talked about how Dave had reaped the seeds of his own youth. Dave had been a handful as a child and teenager with no father for guidance or discipline. By the time he was nine, his mother was ill, no longer able to work in the mill. She turned him over to juvenile authorities because she couldn't take care of him and he was always in and out of trouble. He often stole because there was no money or food in the house. In the 1950s, he wandered the streets of Columbus and the banks of the Chattahoochee River like Huck Finn along the Mississippi. For money he took coins from fountains on

Broadway and bought food. The Christmas he was twelve he lived with a foster family with two daughters and two sons of their own. Dave and the two brothers received new coats for Christmas. But the two brothers also received new gloves. Dave wanted new gloves, too. He remedied the situation at Sears, lifting his own.

But understanding Patrick's behavior was often difficult. He had lacked nothing except discipline from his mother and her family in Dave's absence. Dave had at times over-disciplined or, out of guilt for being away from his son more often than he liked, allowed Patrick too much leeway. Dave had done all he could to provide materially for his son and always said, "I love you." Things he had lacked in his own childhood.

When Dave lumbered back through the door that day, it was without Patrick.

"Couldn't find him?" Deborah asked.

"Not a sign," he said, charging to the bedroom to change clothes. Moments later when the phone rang, they both raced to answer. "Yes, this is Dave Tainsh. Okay, I'll be right there."

"What is it?" Deborah asked, squeezing a dishtowel in her hands.

"I've gotta get Patrick. He's been stopped by the police riding around with a girl on somebody's motor scooter with a broken tail light and of course, no license."

"I can't believe this!" Deborah shouted in disgust.

Dave returned within the hour, pushing Patrick through the door.

"Get to your room, now!" he shouted. "You're grounded, do you hear me? I'm tired of your shit."

Deborah followed them down the hall. Patrick plopped down on his bed. A poster hung on the wall with a surfer balanced in the curve of a wave, and next to that hung posters of skateboarders from *Thrasher* magazine. Patrick's surfboard and skateboards stood in a corner.

"I want to go back to Virginia Beach. I miss Gramma and the rest of my family."

"Well you're not going back. Get that through your head right now! What do you want to do, live with your mother and that bastard she married so he can beat the hell out of you?"

"No, I'll live with Gramma," Patrick replied in his low tone.

"You are not your grandmother's responsibility, you're mine, and this is where you'll stay. The only reason you want to go back is because no one monitors you there. You don't need to be around those drugs that some of your relatives mess with. That's what's wrong with you now!"

"Well, I'll find a way to go back, I will. I don't want to be here."

"You better watch your mouth, you hear me?" Dave said, standing with his fists clenched at his sides, restraining himself from hitting his son.

Patrick fell silent as Dave turned, marched to the living room, and stared at the television from the sofa.

"What are we going to do?" Deborah cried. "This is driving me nuts. I can't stand all this stress and fighting."

"I don't want to talk now. Leave me alone," Dave snapped at her.

"But we need to discuss this. Why don't you just let him go back? It's been over a year and things are no better. You and I can't even get along anymore. What am I going to do when you go to the field for weeks at a time or back overseas?"

"Listen," Dave said. He had looked at her with an expression cold enough to send alarms to her heart. "No one—no one, will come between me and my son or before my son. He's not going back to Virginia to live. Now leave me alone."

Those words started the path that had eventually pushed her to leave him. But on the day after the incident, he did come to his senses enough to listen to her when she called him at work, saying she'd found a family counselor's name in the Yellow Pages. She'd called the psychologist's number and immediately gone to his office to talk. He had recommended they all come in for family counseling.

After a surprised "You did what?" and a moment of silence, Dave said they would talk after work. By the time he reached home, he had decided the counselor might be a positive step.

At Patrick's request, he met with the counselor alone most times. Although Deborah and Dave never knew what Patrick said, they were pleased that he was comfortable speaking with the psychologist. The counselor called at times to say Patrick was dropping by his office at random just to talk, but he needed their permission to meet with the minor.

"Of course," they said. Though Patrick still pushed the envelope if he wanted something bad enough.

~

Deborah moved a step forward in the Wal-Mart line. She shook her head and smiled as the boys in front of her spoke to each other, laughed, and picked up a can of jerky chew from the rack at the end of the counter. They wore baggy athletic shorts to their knees, much like the surf shorts that Patrick had always worn. Their feet were out of proportion to their pencil thin legs. They pulled their hands through uncombed, shaggy heads, like she'd seen Patrick do so many times. She thought about Patrick and his best friend, Chris, when they all lived in Southern California, how they would have stood around talking and laughing about things important only to them, with no cares or concerns about events going on in the rest of the world. How they lived only for the best waves they could catch in the early mornings off the California coast. Or they schemed how to get Patrick's restriction lifted after Deborah had waited on the sofa on a Friday or Saturday night worrying because he wasn't home by curfew.

Seeing a *Newsweek* magazine in the rack with the picture of a ground soldier with his helmet, rifle, and backpack, Deborah felt a twinge of mixed pride and sorrow. Patrick was no longer the lanky, shaggy-headed teenager or defiant young man; he was a man with combat gear preparing to follow behind the first wave of ground soldiers who had already invaded Iraq.

~ FIVE ~

MOMENTS AFTER DEBORAH had driven away toward Wal-Mart, Dave jogged to answer the ringing phone inside the garage. He checked his watch. It was 10:15 a.m. Checking caller ID and grabbing the receiver, he said, "Hey, son. What's up?"

"Hey, Dad. We're stepping onto the C-5 headed for Kuwait, then on to Iraq. We'll be attached to the First Marine Expeditionary Force."

"Son, you take care of yourself. We love you. Don't you forget that."

"I love you, too. Tell Deborah I love her. I gotta go."

"Write as soon as you can when you get there."

"I will. I'll call as soon as I can."

"Okay, Son, we love you. Bye."

Dave walked back to the yard with a cigarette in his fingers. *God, please take care of my boy,* he pleaded. *Take care of my boy.*

As soon as Deborah reached the house, Dave told her about the call.

"I can't believe I missed talking to him." Deborah hugged her arms around her husband's waist, placed the side of her face against his chest. "There's no telling when we'll hear from him again."

"I know," Dave said, returning her hug. "He said tell you he loves you. He'll write or call as soon as he can."

In the kitchen, Deborah wrote on the whiteboard attached to the front of the refrigerator: *Pat dep: 10:15 a.m. 4-1-03.* It would never be erased.

Three weeks later, sleeping on the sofa with help from Tylenol PM, Deborah jumped when the phone rang. It was four a.m. She fumbled for the lamp switch while grabbing the phone's receiver.

"Hello," she said, trying to focus on the caller ID.

"Deborah!" she heard the sound of Patrick's voice from the other side of the world.

"Hey, where are you?"

"Baghdad—Saddam City."

Static in the line caused Patrick's words to break up.

"So what are you doing?"

"Weapons confiscation."

"Hold on while I get your dad before the line breaks."

Deborah rushed down the dark hall to the bedroom. "Honey, wake up, Patrick's on the phone. He's calling from Baghdad." Dave grabbed the bedside receiver from Deborah's hand and told her to return to the extension.

"Hey son! How are you? We love you."

"Love you, too," Patrick said.

"How are you feeling?"

"Tired. It's been a tough road. We're destroying weapons and fighting the Feydayeen."

"How are you making this call?" Dave asked.

"The sergeant major's letting us use his phone."

"It made me mad," Dave said, "when you called Kacee and didn't call your family first. Is it love?"

"He's just kidding," Deborah interjected from the phone in the family room.

Kacee, still waiting to leave for Afghanistan, had called the day before to say that Patrick had reached her. He had arrived in country okay and asked her to call to let them know he was doing well. "I guess it is," Patrick said. Deborah and Dave laughed.

The connection began to fade, finally going dead. Deborah placed the receiver in its cradle, walked back to the bedroom and sat on the bed. Moments later the phone rang again. She handed the phone directly to Dave as he sat up again.

"Hey son, have you received any packages yet? There's three or four floating around out there with some letters."

"Not yet," Patrick told him.

"Well what's going on where you are?"

"They've got us working twenty-hour days. We had to come to Baghdad to pick up a truck."

"How are the civilians acting toward you?"

"Mixed," Patrick said. "I'd better go, there are others waiting to use the phone."

Dave placed the phone close to Deborah's ear. As she said, "I love you," the connection died.

"Thank God, he's okay," Deborah said, kissing her husband on the side of his face.

Dave returned the kiss, then rolled off the side of the bed and pulled his robe on.

"Yeah, it was good to hear from him. Why don't you get back to sleep? I'm getting up."

Dave went outside in the pre-dawn morning for a smoke while his wife fell back to sleep. For now, he was calmed, along with Deborah, to know Patrick was able to make a call home at least once a week.

~ SIX ~

BY THE MIDDLE OF MAY, oaks, maples, and hickories had christened the month with an explosion of green and the smell of cascading lavender wisteria that drifted from the dense wooded landscape.

Deborah stretched from sleep and ambled to the kitchen where she found a note on the table from Dave. It was 9:30. He was off to Wal-Mart for a phone card to mail to Patrick. After pouring coffee into the cup left by her husband next to the coffee pot, she walked to the back porch and sat down in her favorite rocker. A hummingbird, a symbol of beauty and love found in American Indian lore, darted back and forth to the feeder. Deborah looked in the direction of dry leaves rustling beyond the deck. She saw the doe, which often visited the backyard, edging her way toward the bucket that Deborah kept filled with corn. The deer hesitated a moment and twitched her short tail; her warm, almond eyes met Deborah's as two fawns appeared still wearing their spots.

"If only the world were this beautiful everywhere," Deborah thought. "If only we could place a protective net over all we love."

Although e-mail or a phone call came weekly from Iraq, Patrick never left her mind. *What is he doing right now?* she wondered.

She slid her fingers across Patrick's regimental motto, *Toujours Pret, Always Ready,* on her sweatshirt. She had bought the shirt during Dave's and her visit to Fort Polk. Proud to be an Army scout, Patrick had taken them on a tour of the cavalry museum.

~

"The Dragoons are the oldest continuously serving regiment in the U.S. Army," he told them. "They were founded in 1836 by order of President Andrew Jackson to fight the Seminole Indians."

He explained his shoulder sleeve insignia, a gold eight-pointed star of rays, surmounted by a green palmetto leaf, charged with a silver fleur-de-lis and a green ribbon scroll. On this was the regimental motto, *Toujours Pret*.

"The fleur-de-lis is the historic emblem of France," Patrick said. "The Second Cavalry Regiment was the only American unit that participated as a horse cavalry in France during World War I." Listening to Patrick with pride, they walked past the statue of a chestnut quarter horse.

Deborah had not been surprised at all by Patrick's ability to tell the history of his unit. Although he had disliked school, he loved history, along with geography and science. She would never forget helping him with a report when he was in the ninth grade.

"I've got to do a paper on Oswald and Kennedy," Patrick told her one evening after she arrived home from work.

"Well, do you need some help? Do we need to go to the library or bookstore?"

"You don't mind helping me?" Patrick seemed surprised.

"Not at all. How about we work on it over the weekend?"

On Saturday, with Patrick's history book, they sat together looking at photos. Deborah pointed to the one of Kennedy and the first lady waving from the back of a convertible in Houston.

"I remember exactly where I was when that was happening," Deborah said.

"Oh yeah. Where? How old were you?"

"I was eight years old and in the third grade in Woodland, Georgia," she told him. "In a room full of third, fourth, and fifth graders during a music class. The teacher turned on a black and white television, and there it was. The president waving and then slumping."

Deborah always liked to believe that Patrick had enjoyed, as much as she did, working on projects and hearing her stories. Though their past had presented strained moments, she was sure they cared deeply for one another. On an afternoon during the visit at Fort Polk she had told him how proud she was of his decisions. She'd never forget what he said to her.

"I know I caused a lot of problems. I just didn't believe back then that anyone could treat me good and mean it. Or hound me to stay on a clean track because they loved me. It just took me a long time to figure it out."

Deborah smiled and said, "That's okay. Look where we are and what you're doing now."

At the museum that day, Deborah declared her need for a sweatshirt. She left with the one she now wore with pride. She had teased him saying, "You finally found your niche, didn't you, *dude?*"

"Yeah, I'm not a floundering fool anymore," he laughed. "I like romping around in the Louisiana swamps."

~

Dave's truck engine brought Deborah from her thoughts. The doe and fawns bolted into the mass of trees and disappeared into the brush.

"Hey beautiful, after forty-nine days look what we got." Dave stepped onto the porch with two envelopes in his hand.

"Let me see!" Deborah said, grabbing them from her husband. She read from the earliest date.

> *Hey.*
> *It's April 7, 2003 0424 Zulu and we are sitting at Al Salem Iraqi Air Base. That's 7 km away from Nasariyah. I have a little time so I thought I would write. We've been in Iraq for two days now. Light resistance on the way here and nothing but sand and mud built shacks. The majority of the people greet us with open arms. But there are those who hate us. I'm doing good. This morning US forces entered downtown Baghdad. We cheered with motivation on that. Today we push North on a recon. It's weird, Dad, to be at war. These people*

are so oppressed that to see the kids living like this hurts. I cried the other day when two kids asked for food and I couldn't give it to them. We are very close to Baghdad and sometimes you can hear the bombers overhead. I am glad to be here with these guys. They are really good men. Aside from lack of sleep we are doing well. Please do me a favor and call Kacee and tell her I'm thinking about her and I miss her. Please do that for me. Tell everyone there that I said hi and I miss them. I just want you to know that I love you and Deborah very much. Gotta go. Write back.

Love,
Patrick

Hey.

It's the 10th of April 0700 zulu. Right now we are stationary in Central Iraq not too far from Baghdad. We had a mission yesterday vs. the Bathe party occupied village and took 14 pows with casualties. That's all I can say about that. We are advancing very rapidly with aggressiveness. It's really awesome to see a Cavalry troop work and win. We were with Marines for a while but we've been alone for about 2 1/2 days. Everyone is doing their job well and the commander is very pleased. I can't tell you where we are but we are close. The region isn't desert, it's like a tropical region of the country-- palm trees, vegetation, and rivers. The people are very friendly and welcome us with open arms. They want to give us gifts. But we don't take anything. Everywhere we've been has been that way—firefights—then liberate the village— regroup, then move on. From what we hear, the regime is gone. But militia is still here. That's who we encounter. Other than that I'm good. I haven't gone to sleep in about three days and have started a beard in lack of time for hygiene. We've been through two huge dust storms since we've been here. It's not that hot, about like California. Cigarettes are still holding up. Almost 5 cartons left. I traded a Marlboro to an Elder yesterday for an Iraqi made cigarette and it was o.k. He

*wanted me to take the whole pack but I insisted he take mine
which he did. He said 'American, American' and was very
happy. They really want us here. You can see it in their eyes.
They are very affectionate and appreciative chanting Bush
Bush. Well that's about it for now. I gotta go. They are telling
us to rack out. I'm not gonna miss it this time.*
  Love,
  Patrick

That night Dave willed himself to sleep to the sound of Fox
News on the bedroom television. Deborah lay next to him and
switched the channel to the home decorating station as soon as
she heard her husband's labored breathing. She lay awake into
hours after midnight wondering if Patrick had anything decent
to eat, how much dust he'd swallowed, or how many more hours
he had gone without sleep. Was he sleeping in rain and mud or on
top of a Humvee? And how many close calls was he having that
he'd never tell them about? Patrick was their last and first thought
every day, something not uncommon during his life. Deborah
finally drifted to sleep softly repeating, *God, please take care of
our boy. Please.*

~ SEVEN ~

DAVE CAME AROUND the side of the house asking, "Where's the woman of the house?"

It was early June.

"Hey, you're back," Deborah said from her seat on the ground. Her hands were covered in black soil from planting pink and white impatiens in pots for the deck. Wearing gloves took the feel of the dirt and plants away. She had never given thought to how therapeutic working in the soil could be until these days. Her grandmother had loved planting. When Deborah was small, they'd go to the woods together in early spring and dig up honeysuckles and young dogwoods and bring them back home to plant. Her grandmother's favorite annuals were pansies. Deborah had bought a crate of the mixed colors and planted them in the front of the house last week.

"Did you get the box mailed off?"

Dave took a seat in the rocker. He mailed a care package once a week.

"Sure did. I mailed another phone card with more cigarettes and food snacks he can put in his pack. So, what are your plans today, missy?"

"I thought I'd give Kacee a call and see how she is. Let her know we heard from Patrick again. Then I'm going to the fitness center."

"Well, how about some lunch?"

Deborah grinned. "I guess you must be hungry. Turkey sandwiches okay?"

"Sounds fine with me." Dave threw his spent cigarette into the yard.

Deborah followed her husband back inside the house. After cleaning her hands, she prepared sandwiches and left a message for Kacee to give her a call.

That evening when Deborah answered the phone, Kacee's first words were, "Hey, how y'all doin'? Did Patrick sound okay?"

Deborah told Kacee everything she could remember about the phone call. And passed on a message. "Patrick said tell you he loves you."

Kacee giggled. "I love him, too."

"So, do you know when you're leaving?"

"We have to be at Fort Polk for training in July, then we'll leave the first of August for Afghanistan. I've got to start putting my stuff in storage."

"Will you be able to visit us before you leave?"

"I'm planning on coming to Atlanta to Karon's before the end of the month. If y'all don't mind, I'd like to come by for a day or two after I leave there."

"The door's open," Deborah said. "We'd be heart broken if you didn't."

Two weeks later, on Monday evening, Deborah met Kacee in the driveway, which was lined with blooming azaleas.

"Hey, hon, how ya doin'?"

"I'm great! I didn't even get lost!" she said with her pretty grin. Her dark hair curved short around her ears, ready for her rendezvous with training at Fort Polk and then Afghanistan.

"Hey, girl." Dave said, walking from the back of the house toward Kacee's car.

"Hey, yourself."

Dave hugged Kacee and took her bags. "So, you ready for your trip?"

"As ready as I'm gonna be," Kacee laughed. "We'll leave the first of August for the sand box. I told Patrick I'd let him know when I get there. We hope to get some R&R together at Qatar by October."

"I hope it works out," Deborah told her as they walked into the cool house. "How about a glass of wine?"

"Sounds good, I'm ready to relax a while."

"Well, you know where your room and bath are," Deborah said. "You know this is your other home."

"Sure do," Kacee said, hugging Deborah before going to the guestroom that she and Patrick had shared during the holidays.

On August 4th, Deborah marked the calendar again. Kacee had called to say she was boarding the plane to Afghanistan. The first thing Dave did was check for e-mails from Patrick.

"Patrick wants a Game Boy for his birthday," he laughed. "Says he gets bored on down time. He sends his love."

"When you're done with your note, I'll add something," Deborah said, as she pulled the skillet from the cabinet to start breakfast, wishing that Patrick could be at home for his thirty-third birthday on the 25th. She opened the cabinet door next to the stove to pull out the salt and pepper for the scrambled eggs. Her fingers touched a bottle of hot sauce that Patrick had concocted when he was home in March. All his years as a cook and chef's assistant had taught him a lot about food. The last time he was home, he stood at this stove and showed her the best way to prepare pancakes with no oil in the skillet.

"Just make sure the pan is plenty hot before you pour the batter in," he had said. "Turn the heat down, then let the batter brown around the edges before you flip it over." She had stood next to him while he held the spatula in his hand waiting to turn the pancake. She never forgot her cooking lesson, nor made a bad pancake since.

"I guess we better go shopping and get another package in the mail," Dave said. "He needs some Marlboros, t-shirts, and socks."

Dave wrote Patrick a return message telling him that his order was received.

Deborah added the message that Kacee had called and sent her love. Then she ended with, "You know you're my son and I love you. Stay safe."

~ EIGHT ~

SUMMER PASSED INTO FALL and to Friday evening, October 10th. Darkness spread across the valley and the Tainsh home in Midland. A gentle wind shuffled leaves to the ground as distant thunder accompanied a mild rain.

From his corner of the sofa, Dave switched the television station from Fox News to watch *Jeopardy* with Deborah. When the phone rang, Dave muted the television and grabbed the receiver. Deborah stepped from the kitchen toward the family room. Both hoped it was Patrick since they hadn't spoken with him over the past week. They knew he and Kacee had met for R&R in Qatar on October 6th. They were anxious to hear about their visit together, how they both were doing.

After his initial, "Hello," Dave remained expressionless. Deborah noticed her husband's face growing pale. He'd had a heart attack six years ago. She prayed he wasn't having another. With Patrick in the line of fire twenty-four hours a day, she worried about the stress on her husband as much as she worried for Patrick. Standing in the doorway between the kitchen and family room, she gripped the dishcloth with both hands and watched her husband's solemn expression. Nausea set in her stomach.

In the silence, the clock on the mantle ticked with a loud, one, two time like heavy fingers tapping against wood. Usually she would pick up another extension, but this time, Dave's look said, *don't.* She stood frozen while Dave stared at the table and listened intently.

After moments that moved like drops of resin, Deborah heard her husband speak.

"I'm sorry, son. I know how you feel. Just stay focused. Keep yourself covered and don't take any chances. I know you care about your men, and you want to get them home safe, but you've gotta watch out for yourself, too."

Dave looked toward his wife. He knew she was listening to his every word, down to the ones he always ended with: "We love you son. Keep your head down. Stay safe."

He heard his son's words. "I will. I love you, too. Tell Deborah I love her. I gotta go." Then the click.

"What's wrong?" Deborah asked.

Dave rubbed his hand across the top of his head and sighed.

"He lost a buddy last night. It was his first night back from seeing Kacee in Qatar. There was an ambush in Sadr City. A group of the guys were hit with small arms fire and RPGs. He was called in as backup, but got there too late. He said he pulled Staff Sergeant Swisher from the vehicle, but he couldn't save him. Swisher died in his arms. Another soldier, PFC Silva, died, too. After six months, they were his unit's first casualties. He's shook up pretty bad."

Dave sat with his wife in silence as they grasped each other's hands. Deborah placed her head on her husband's shoulder.

"I need a smoke," Dave finally said. Kissing Deborah on the side of her face, he rose from the sofa. Deborah pulled her journal from the coffee table.

Outside, Dave shoved his lighter back inside his jeans pocket and blew smoke rings into the darkness. Clouds covered the stars. He studied the dark sky, knowing the stars were behind all that darkness, and sooner or later the clouds would move, and the glow of the stars would again be visible. He knew the dark clouds that now enveloped his son's world would, with time, also go away. The worry was what would remain after the clouds disappeared. Stars often burned out. Dave prayed his son wouldn't do the same before his own dark clouds lifted. He knew first-hand what his son was going through. He had picked up enough body parts in Vietnam. For the time being, there were no words to comfort his son. Patrick's prior calls had all been upbeat with no complaints. This time he was full of anxiety. All that Dave felt he could do now was pray that his son could shake off the awful experience and remain focused. It sounded cold. But that's what a soldier had to do to stay alert and alive. He wished he could take his son's place; he wished he could hold the toddler who once wore the blue jumper and size one sneakers in the photo sitting on his desk, the toddler of thirty-two years ago whose arms reached for his dad who, at this moment, felt lost and too far away from his son.

Deborah laid her journal on the coffee table and walked to the garage where Dave stared into the rainy night and puffed another cigarette.

"You okay?" she asked almost in a whisper.

"I'm just thinking about my boy," Dave said.

"I know. Me, too. I know that losing a friend is hard on him. It makes this war much more real."

"I just hope he doesn't lose his focus," Dave told her. "Losing a buddy can rattle him if he lets it."

The rain continued a gentle tap against the shedding trees and the roof of the house. Deborah stepped closer to her husband, placing her arm around his waist.

"Well, I know he's enough like his dad to hang in and do what he needs to do," she said. "He'll be fine." Deborah knew she had to remain positive.

"I hope you're right," Dave said. "I hope you're right."

Even if he wanted to share them with his wife, Dave had no way to describe his thoughts. And he had no words for the pride he felt. Patrick never whined about his job. His call tonight had been the first time Dave had heard anxiety in his son's voice.

From that night, Dave printed out all the e-mail messages that followed at least every other day with notes as simple as, "I'm O.K."

On October 11th, at Bagram, Afghanistan, the night sky glowed in the way that can only be seen in a desert. Like the bluest diamonds shining through ebony velvet, a rich, calm beauty sparkled across the heavens, ignoring despair crossing the earth, as though proving there *was* something better.

Kacee was still on a high after returning the day before from seeing Patrick in Qatar. She looked at the time on her wristwatch. It was nine p.m. as she left her quarters and returned to her office to check for any e-mail messages that Patrick may have sent since returning to Baghdad two days ago. She found none.

I guess you're busy tonight, she thought, looking at Patrick's photo taped to the wall next to her desk. He was standing in the foreground of the blue waters of the Persian Gulf in Qatar. She'd taken the digital photo during their visit together. *Well, I'm tired, babe. I'm going to bed; maybe we'll catch each other tomorrow. Goodnight. I love you.*

Kacee strolled back across the dusty ground toward her tent. She thought about the night before. She and Patrick had spent an hour conversing via the computers and instant message before Patrick left for patrol. He had told her he wanted to be married after they were both stateside. They talked back and forth about where he might be based once he was back home, and how she could possibly get a teaching job with a school on a military base.

Back inside her tent, Kacee noticed her bunkmate, Alice, already asleep. Sitting down on her cot, she unlaced her boots. Her feet ached along with her head. She and Alice had handled a lot of paperwork and processing today. They had worked late to keep a handle on all the activity going on with the unit.

Too tired to walk back to the showers, she washed her face and refreshed her skin with baby wipes. She would shower and wash her hair in the morning. After changing from utilities to sweats, she shut off the light hanging overhead and stretched out on the cot. Thinking about Patrick and what he had said about getting married, she drifted to the previous March, seven months ago, when he had wanted to call off their relationship.

~

Patrick had stopped by her apartment en route from Fort Polk to see his parents in Georgia. She was going to ride along for the visit, but to her surprise he said he needed to go alone; he needed to think. He finally said he didn't believe they should consider themselves a couple while he was in Iraq. He didn't want her to worry about him.

They had spent hours talking, but Patrick was gone the next morning before she awoke. After that, she decided to let go without holding anything against him. After all, earlier in their relationship, she had broken up with him because of her own insecurities, afraid to keep the relationship going for fear she'd get her heart broken like it had been ten years before when her husband left her for someone else. But Patrick had talked with her, listened to her reasons, and then patiently waited for her to reconsider.

To keep her mind off Patrick's visit and leaving during the night, she decided to focus on other things. At the same time Patrick was preparing to ship out, she was waiting for word to report to Fort Polk with her Guard unit to train for Afghanistan. That meant making arrangements for moving and storing her personal goods while she was deployed. And she always had plenty to do for her first grade class, or there were movies and dinners she could share with girlfriends. And that's where she was headed, two weeks after Patrick's visit, when she answered her ringing cell phone and heard that soft, easy voice saying, "Hey, how ya doin?"

The conversation and the rest of that night would never leave her.

"I'm okay," she said. "I'm getting ready to meet Kat for dinner." It was four-thirty in the afternoon.

"Well, I just wanted to let you know we're pushing out tomorrow. I didn't know if I could see you before we leave. I can't leave the base, but I thought you might drive over. I know it's asking a lot, but I'd really love to see you."

"I really can't. I have dinner plans and then there's work in the morning."

"I understand. No problem. You take care of yourself."

"You, too," she told him, and hung up before she changed her mind.

At the restaurant Kat sensed that Kacee's mind was somewhere in the distance. "Okay girl, what's wrong?" she asked.

"Oh God, Kat. Patrick called and wanted me to see him tonight. He's pushing out tomorrow for Kuwait."

"Girl, you better go. That man loves you and you love him. Don't just keep sitting here."

"You're right, I've gotta go, I've just got to." Kacee hugged Kat and ran for the door. It was already seven p.m., and the drive took four hours. She didn't even have a renewed military I.D. How would she find him once she got to Fort Polk? The guards might not let her on base. She tried to call Patrick on his cell phone, but as usual, he didn't have it on. With no other idea, she called Dave and Deborah's.

When the phone rang, Dave answered to hear her anxious voice.

"Dave, this is Kacee. If Patrick calls tell him I'm on the way. Tell him I'll drive straight to his barracks. I feel awful. He called earlier and asked me to come and I said no, it was too far to have to turn around and come back. But tell him I'm on the way." Dave promised he would.

She arrived at the base just before midnight and with a little begging and explaining the situation, the guards let her through. It had helped that she was in the Guard. She made her way to the barracks and parked where Patrick could see her car lights. When she stepped from the car, he was already waiting. She would never forget that kiss and his words.

"I'm sorry," he told her. "I was so confused about everything with me having to leave. If something happens to me, I don't want you to have to hurt again like when you lost your dad. All this is so hard. We just don't know what's going to happen."

"Well, that's just the chance we'll have to take," she told him.

And she never regretted making that drive even though she didn't get back home until five a.m., and had only an hour of sleep before dressing for work.

~

Seven months passed before Kacee saw him again. She was thankful they had managed to coordinate to meet for R&R at Camp As Sayliyah, the place many referred to as the Club Med of the Middle East. Located in Qatar on the outskirts of the capital city, Doha, it was the world's largest pre-positioning site for the Army. The United States could send troops there and issue all the equipment needed to have soldiers ready for war.

Added to Camp As Sayliyah was what the military called the Fighter Management Program, a place where troops could get away from the stress of combat for a few days. Soldiers from Operation Enduring Freedom and Operation Iraqi Freedom had access to weight rooms, golf, tennis, scuba diving, a swimming pool, and scheduled trips around Qatar that included pristine beaches and camel races. They even had access to cable television with about ten English channels that included CNN International, Star Movies, and Disney. Of course all the channels were screened daily to "satisfy all tastes and censored to adhere to the local culture" as the Central Command's information pack stated. There was also a list of do's and don'ts. Everyone had to keep in mind not to cross their feet in a way that would expose the bottoms of their feet, which was considered an insult in Muslim countries. Soldiers were also told not to receive items with their left hand, or eat with the fingers of their left hand, because Muslims hold that the left hand is reserved for bodily functions. Men and women had to dress appropriately, wearing shorts and sleeveless tops only at the beach and around the pool. And there could be no public displays of affection; not even holding hands was permitted.

Seeing Patrick again had meant another late night ride, but this time on a bus and through the desert. Kacee kept checking her watch, waiting for the bus to reach the entrance of the camp.

At the gate, the bus slowed to maneuver past concrete security barricades. It was ten minutes after midnight. She bit her bottom lip. Beneath her breath she kept saying, *Let's go,* and *Please, God, let him be there. Please, please, please.*

Patrick had promised to wait for her until midnight, outside the beer tent. Otherwise he would see her the next morning at the pool. Approaching the drop off point, the bus slowed to a stop. Kacee looked through the bus windows, her eyes racing from one spot to another before seeing him. Patrick was sitting on the concrete ledge in front of a brick wall. He was wearing jeans and the striped multi-colored shirt he had worn at his parents' house last Christmas, the same shirt he wore in the picture that each of them carried, Kacee sitting in his lap and his chin propped on top of her head.

Dragging her camouflage bag to her shoulder, Kacee waited for a spot to enter the aisle. After the bus door opened, she hit the ground running. Dropping her bag before she reached Patrick, rules or not, she hugged him and placed a quick peck on his lips.

Like small balls of white fire, the stars glowed in the midnight sky that night. Kacee wasn't sure what to say. Talking on the phone and e-mailing one another had been so natural. But after seven months with no physical contact, she felt shy and bashful.

After getting her room key, Kacee changed from her military utilities to jeans and a shirt. There was too little time to take a shower. She brushed out her hair and sprayed her body with lavender scent from Victoria's Secret. It was one of Patrick's favorites. Outside her quarters, Patrick waited. With the beer tent closed, they walked together around the area Patrick had scoped before her arrival.

"Hey, let's go in here," he suggested, slipping past a guard to enter a bunker. "At least we can have some privacy for a while."

Inside the bunker, Patrick adjusted a number of sandbags to sit on. Kacee remembered how he began pouring himself out to her. She had listened, not knowing what to say. He lay with his head in her lap and his eyes closed as she gently rubbed her fingers across his forehead and examined his face. Looking at him that night, all she thought was, *what a man.* For six months, as a gunner on the top of a Humvee, he had seen war in Iraq close up, down to knowing his number of kills and making tough decisions.

"I thought I was going to have to kill a kid who was aiming an RPG at us," he told her. Instead, I shot over his head to scare him away. I just couldn't kill a kid."

He smoked another cigarette. All the sleepless hours, living on the edge, and never knowing whom to trust showed in the weight he'd lost, in the hollowness she'd seen in his eyes. But in his e-mails and phone calls to her he always encouraged her to do her best and not let things get her down.

Her problems with a jerk boss and a prissy kid who wouldn't carry her own workload at Bagram suddenly seemed trivial. All she had to do was process Article Fifteens that lowered a soldier's rank or took away pay for not following orders, not worry about snipers and twelve-year-olds with rocket propelled grenades. She had experienced only one scare, which she told Patrick about.

It was the night in Bagram when she and her bunkmate, Alice, were awakened by a whistling sound and then a boom. Everyone at Bagram usually felt pretty safe from direct attacks. The fighting was in the mountains with Special Forces. She always felt grateful to the soldiers who came into camp filthy with long hair and beards after weeks without baths, looking themselves like huge rugged mountain men. But that night had left her rattled. In their monthly, spring, and summer Guard training, they had trained in the woods of Fort Polk, Louisiana, not in a desert environment. They had trained for how and when to use their MOP suits in case of chemical and germ warfare. But they had not received training on the sounds of incoming mortars or RPGs.

"What do we do?" she'd asked Alice, as they both jumped from their cots and scrambled to get to a light and put on their flak jackets.

"Get the hell outta here," Alice said as they grabbed their helmets and M-16s.

Then they heard the "Big Voice in the Sky" as they called it. The white blimp with cameras saying, "This is not a test, this is not a test." While most of the soldiers headed for bunkers, Kacee and Alice had to run to the S1 building to make an accountability report to ensure no one was missing from their unit. They were lucky. Only one soldier couldn't be accounted for. Unauthorized, he had been outside the camp using a telephone. As a legal specialist, Kacee later prepared the paperwork for his Article Fifteen.

After exchanging stories, Patrick had pulled her to him, kissed her the way she wanted. Sitting on the sandbags, they made love, a memory that, tonight, Kacee drifted to sleep with, holding the t-shirt she kept under her pillow, while Patrick, hundreds of miles away in Baghdad, headed out with Eagle Troop on his nightly scouting mission, minus two men.

~ NINE ~

BY DECEMBER, PATRICK was excited about Saddam's capture in Tikrit.

"We're kicking butt," he said.

Then he put in his Christmas request.

"Hey, I'd like to have a digital camera for Christmas. That way I can send pictures home."

The next day Deborah wandered with Dave through the mall and selected a digital camera.

"Kacee said she and her bunkmates need some lotions, shampoos, and hot hair conditioners," Deborah told her husband. "I'll walk over to the beauty supply shop while you roam around in here."

Deborah walked from Circuit City to Trade Secretz where shelves were loaded with hair and skin products. She was deciding which ones to buy when she heard a familiar voice say, "Merry Christmas."

Deborah turned to the smiling face of Rose Hendrix.

"Merry Christmas to you, too! How are you?"

Rose and Deborah had spoken several times since both Patrick and Rose's son had left for Iraq.

"Have you heard from Christian lately?" Deborah asked.

"Yeah, he seems to be doing fine. If he's not, he's not letting me know anything. How about Patrick?"

"Thank goodness, he's still okay. We hear from him at least once a week."

"What are you two talking about?" Dave walked next to Deborah.

"Hey, big guy. We're just updating each other on the latest with the boys. How are you holding up?"

"A day at a time. How about you?"

"Oh, I'll have scabs and calluses on my knees by the time Christian gets home."

"I know what you mean," Deborah grinned.

"Well, I gotta run. Daddy's waiting for me to take him to lunch."

"Call if you need us," Dave said, giving Rose a hug and waving her off.

Deborah loaded containers on the counter for the cashier while Dave waited to help carry bags to the car.

The next morning, with everything packed in the regulation-size boxes, Dave mailed the goods to Baghdad and Afghanistan. In Patrick and Kacee's absence, to keep the Christmas spirit, Dave helped Deborah set up the full Christmas toy land. He set up the deer and candy canes with white lights on the hill in front of the house. The ten-foot Christmas tree glowed in front of the dining room windows.

"I'm not taking the tree down until you're home," Deborah told Patrick the next time he called. "You'll have gifts waiting." Deborah took plenty of photos with her digital camera and sent them to Patrick and Kacee through e-mail.

Deborah wrote a note to Patrick and attached the group picture of Dave, Sindy, and Jason in front of the fireplace. They wore "We Got Him" t-shirts with the bearded face of Saddam Hussein behind jail bars.

"I have a shirt like this for you when you get home," she told him.

Though they tried dimming the truth with humor, Deborah and Dave both knew that the fall of Baghdad and the capture of Saddam would not protect U.S. and coalition soldiers from continued injury or loss of life. They heard the daily news about factions and terrorists still attacking the troops with rocket propelled grenades and roadside bombs. They also knew that as a cavalry scout, Patrick patrolled streets around Baghdad in a Humvee convoy and searched neighborhoods. He and the other soldiers searched suspicious vehicles, confiscated weapon caches, and suppressed suspicious individuals who could stir continued trouble. Patrick also manned a fifty-caliber weapon on top of the commanding officer's vehicle. He was considered one of the best, his reputation always preceding him from one commander to another. His unit's final destination and camp was Baghdad International Airport, which they guarded from insurgents.

Patrick responded to Deborah's e-mail and group photo with, "I love it!"

And with everything going on around him, he managed to locate and mail home a Christmas card.

Deborah set it on the mantle. The cover words read:

For the Greatest Parents Ever! The inside verse said: *Thinking of you both, knowing that you've always been there with love and caring and always when you were needed.*

Dave also received a December birthday greeting with a picture of a dad and small son walking together, the card said:

Dad, you've always been my hero. Nothing was beyond your reach to fix or do. Now that I'm older, more grounded to earth, you're still my hero and the kind of person I want to be.

Deborah kept it standing on Dave's desk.

On Christmas Eve the phone rang at nine p.m. It was five a.m., Christmas morning in Iraq. Dave answered with, "Merry Christmas, Son. How you doing?"

"Well, not everyone can say they spent a Christmas at Baghdad International," Patrick joked, keeping things on the light side as always.

Deborah picked up the extension. "Hey you, did you get your gift box?"

"Sure did. I'll get some photos back to you as soon as I can."

"Well, you sound good. Are you guys getting a big meal today?"

"We're supposed to. But I'd just enjoy some extra sleep. And I'm ready to be home so I can take a hot shower every day."

"Well, you don't have long now. Just keep yourself safe. I love you," Deborah said.

"I love you, too."

"I'm handing the phone to Jason. He and Sindy want to talk to you."

Sindy grabbed the phone. "Hey dork, get your butt home. We miss you."

Deborah listened from her corner of the sofa while Jason and Sindy joked, trying to keep the reality of their family's life out of view.

After Jason and Sindy told Patrick that they'd see him later, Dave spoke his usual closing words.

"Keep your head down, son. We love you. Call back when you can."

On New Year's Eve, Deborah sat close to her husband as they watched New York's festivities on television. She couldn't help but think how last year their "kids" had all celebrated together. And now, Patrick and Kacee were miles apart and under fire instead of laughing with Jason and Sindy.

Snuggling closer, Deborah and Dave counted backward from ten while the Waterford crystal ball slid to the ground at Times Square. In America, the cost had risen to protect the New Year's Eve party-goers, who mingled with secret patrols and unseen rooftop snipers while Lady Liberty sought restoration in the harbor.

Last June Deborah and Dave had visited Ground Zero at Liberty and Church Streets in Manhattan, the place Deborah referred to as "proof of no guarantees." The sun shown so bright that day, it seemed a symbol that all would be well. She had stood with her fingers curled into the chain link fence that surrounded the massive gaping hole. The place where foundations and walls had disintegrated and fallen into rubble after the jets, fuel, ash, and black smoke of 9-11 brought terror to the nation, and more so to those caught inside and near the Twin Towers where the destruction pulled eyes of the world like magnets to television screens and left Americans to live with color-coded terrorist alerts.

At the site, an entry ramp led to the scourged ground and an iron cross stood burned in place to remember all those who had been lost. Deborah had taken photos of the area and sent them to Patrick and Kacee. This was the reason they and thousands of other soldiers were sitting daily on a seat with death in Iraq and Afghanistan. They had both told her they kept the photos close to remind them of why they were committed to their jobs.

Yes, Deborah thought to herself, *everyone at home in the U.S. could go on enjoying their party favors knowing they have the best in the world holding the line of defense thousands of miles away on this 2003 New Year's Eve night.*

After the crystal ball came to the ground in New York, Dave changed the station to *The Tonight Show* in Los Angeles, where Jay Leno popped a bottle of champagne. Deborah turned toward her husband and kissed him into the New Year in Georgia, where they continued to busy their way through each day, holding their breaths for Patrick's and Kacee's every call and e-mail.

~ TEN ~

"I WONDER IF PATRICK would like to go to Disney World when he gets home?" Deborah was looking through a travel book at the various resorts close to the Disney theme parks in Orlando. "I think it'd be a lot of fun to take a family trip."

"He said he wanted to go to any resort we could find," Dave said. He was pushing back in his recliner to watch the *O'Reilly Factor* when the phone rang.

"Looks like Patrick," he said when he saw the caller ID.

Dave heard his son's cheery voice. "Hey Dad, I'm countin' the days! We're on the backside, now. Word is we'll be headed for Kuwait by mid-March and home by April."

"Well it's only the 10th of February. Just stay focused until you're out of there. Don't lose your edge. It ain't over until you hit the USA."

"I know, Dad. Don't worry."

"We're going to Disney World when you get home," Deborah said, holding the extension.

"Sounds like a winner to me. I'm ready to be anywhere but here for a while."

"Just hang in there, bud," Dave repeated. "Just keep your head on straight. And don't forget how much we love you."

"Me, too, Dad. I gotta go. Tell everybody I love and miss 'em. I'll call you later."

Dave placed the phone back in its cradle, as Deborah wrote *Pat called* on the calendar, never thinking it would be the last time they'd ever speak to their son.

Two days later, after watching television until two o'clock in the morning, Deborah fell asleep on the sofa. By six a.m. she was awake, thinking she must have dreamt that someone was pounding on the door. Looking toward the window next to the fireplace she saw it was still dark. She was turning on her side to return to sleep when she heard the pounding again. This time she heard a male voice calling for Sergeant Major Tainsh.

She felt muddled, but finally realized she wasn't dreaming. For a split moment the thought crossed her mind that it was one of Dave's former Marines pulling an early morning prank. After eighteen years, some of them had contacted him a few weeks earlier. In the old days in California, there were times when one or two of them would knock on the door looking for a place to sleep to keep from driving on the base after drinking a few beers. Hearing the bold knock again, Deborah threw off her blanket.

"Do you hear somebody banging on the door?" she called down the hall to her husband.

Having shifted abruptly into a sitting position, she felt nauseated. Her face turned cool, as though all the blood were rushing to her toes. Suddenly, with a pang of fright, her insides became a mass of jitters. She didn't want to move. When the knock sounded again, she shouted, "Just a minute" toward the door, and waited for Dave to come down the hall.

Dave had also thought he was dreaming until he heard his wife's voice. Alarmed, and trying to wake from a deep sleep, he pulled on his robe while yelling back to Deborah that he was on the way.

They reached the foyer entrance at the same time. Dave carried the pistol that stayed under the bed.

"What the hell?" he said as they approached the front door.

They lived in a nice section of the county, outside of town where nothing out of the ordinary ever happened. But there was always the first time, and Dave Tainsh wasn't one to take unusual occurrences lightly. Deborah flipped the switches that turned on the foyer and front yard lights. Looking out the long narrow window beside the door, all that Dave could say was, "Oh, hell," and began shaking as Deborah repeated, "No, God, no," over and over again.

There was only one reason for two men in Army dress greens to be standing at the door in the still dark morning. They were bringing a horrid message not worthy of sunlight. But this couldn't be possible. Just yesterday Dave had called Allstate to reinstate Patrick's car insurance. He had mailed a check to Fort Polk to the captain's wife to help buy soap and shaving cream to put in the barracks for the guys when they arrived home next month. But at that moment, Deborah knew death had truly appeared at their door like a thief in the night. It was 6:00 a.m., February 12th, 2004.

During the notification officer's announcement, "Sir, I'm sorry to inform you…," Deborah's mind replayed a flood of memories. She and Dave had just discussed the trip to Fort Polk to meet the unit when they arrived in another fifty days or so. They had planned the trip to Disney World. The Christmas tree was still in front of the dining room windows with Patrick's gifts beneath it. Now, was someone actually telling them the sun would no longer rise? That overnight, the earth had stopped spinning on its axis? That gravity no longer existed? Deborah fell to her knees on the floor, her hands cupped to her face, catching the flood of tears. Dave stood in silence, his arms crossed in front of his chest as though the posture would repel the horrible truth.

The notification officer continued with, "I'm so sorry," finally breaking the insane moments by asking, gently, if he and the chaplain could possibly come in.

Dave reached his hand to Deborah's, lifting her from her knees. Looking up to see her husband's face white as chalk, she grabbed his arm. Finally finding the words, she said, "I'm sorry, please come inside."

Dave stretched the door open.

"We knew why you were here the moment we saw you," Deborah said.

"Ma'am, I'm so sorry. This is the most difficult part of my job."

The subdued chaplain and the notification officer, a young sergeant, removed their garrison caps, entered the foyer, and walked toward the family room. Deborah felt as though she and Dave were floating inside a bubble that would pop any moment, and the clock's hands would spin backwards. She examined her husband's chalky face, looking for signs of chest pains. After he and the two other men finally took seats, all she could think to do was make coffee for the three of them.

Wiping her swollen eyes and moving like a robot toward the kitchen, she knew she had to call Jason. After starting the coffee, she picked up the portable phone from the counter to dial his number. While watching the steady drip of coffee, she listened to several rings before her son answered his phone.

"We need you here at the house. It's Patrick." She said as calm as possible.

"Mama, what's wrong?' Jason said in his raspy, early morning voice.

"Just come over, and drive careful."

After placing the receiver back in its cradle, Deborah returned to the family room.

From his seat in the corner of the sofa, Dave finally found his voice. "What happened? And when?"

The chaplain, seated in the chair at the corner of the sofa where Dave sat, played nervously with his garrison cap. In the chair at the opposite end of the sofa, the young sergeant sat holding a manila folder.

The chaplain spoke. "It was an IED, sir, a roadside bomb. The unit was in convoy on a patrol in western Baghdad. We were told it occurred about twenty-two hundred hours, or ten p.m., last night."

"He wasn't supposed to be on more patrols. He was getting ready to come home." Dave gazed at the floor, disbelieving the words he heard.

"Sir, I'm so sorry," the chaplain said, with the soft voice of a man of the cloth.

For some reason, Deborah figured the time difference. It would have been around two p.m. at home. While she read to children at one of the schools, while Dave took in Fox News, their son had taken his last breaths. At some point in time before this morning, a banner had probably run at the bottom of the television saying, "Two soldiers killed today in western Baghdad, names withheld until notification of next of kin."

Deborah watched her husband, fearing where his state of mind might lead as he continued staring into the floor, as though burning a hole through it. She remembered the gun he had brought to the door. She walked to the dining room and found it on the chair where he had left it. Placing a throw blanket over the pistol, she took it to the back of the house and hid it in her closet. She returned to the family room, knowing it was up to her to get her husband through this.

With only dull lamp light in the large room and the sun still below the horizon, there was a thick oozing ugliness that couldn't be touched, only felt, draped heavily inside the room, consuming the bodies searching for words that didn't exist to answer questions or bring comfort. Deborah didn't know what a stun gun felt like, but nothing could be worse than the feeling that hovered in this room.

The sergeant finally spoke. The papers he held shook in his hands. "Sir, I understand you're Sergeant Tainsh's sole beneficiary, that his mother is deceased."

"Yes. She died when he was young," Dave responded, meeting the young man's eyes.

"Sir, then, if I could have you confirm the names and spelling on these forms and sign them, we can begin working on the death and burial benefits."

This can't be happening, Deborah kept thinking as she handed her husband his glasses. She watched the paper shake in Dave's hands. If there were ever a moment in her life where she felt outside her body, watching the most horrible scene that could ever occur involving those she loved, this was it.

She watched her husband force the black government pen across the designated lines, leaving his signature in small jerky cursive that resembled a child's.

With the forms completed, Deborah called Rose Hendrix. "Rose, this is Deborah Tainsh. I think we need you. We lost Patrick last night."

Rose hesitated a moment as though she hadn't heard correctly. Then she spoke.

"Oh, God, no, Deborah, this can't be right. I'll be right there. I'll do all I can."

Setting the receiver down, Deborah thought about how to best contact Patrick's grandmother, now in Miami, relatives in North Carolina, friends in California, and Kacee in Afghanistan. She supposed the Red Cross could help with notifications to Miami and Bagram.

Seeing the full coffee pot, she poured three cups of coffee, placed them on a tray and took them into the family room. Offering the chaplain a cup, he smiled, saying, "You're not supposed to be doing things for me. I'm here for you."

"Just pray us through this," Deborah said.

While Deborah handed the cups to her husband and the sergeant, the chaplain walked to the family photo table where he picked up a picture of Patrick standing beside a Humvee in Baghdad.

"He's a handsome young man. I know you're proud of him."

"Yes sir, we are," Dave said.

"I'd like to pray with you."

At that moment, Deborah heard the back door open. Jason and Sindy entered the house from the garage, their eyes red and swollen.

"This ain't happening, I know it's not," Jason cried, hugging Deborah, then his stepfather. Deborah watched him move toward Patrick's eight-by-ten military photo that hung on the wall with years of other family photos. Tears flowed down her son's face as he gritted his teeth. With his muscular arms to his sides and fists folded tight, she knew he wanted to hit something.

"We just talked to him a couple of days ago," Sindy said, wiping her eyes with the back of her hand. "I can't believe this. He was coming home in a few more weeks."

Deborah reached her hand toward Sindy's. "I know," she said. "The chaplain would like to say a few words."

Jason moved next to Sindy. Deborah sat down next to her husband as the gray dawn swallowed the morning darkness and the chaplain, holding Patrick's photo, prayed.

Hours later and sleeping peacefully, Kacee thought she was dreaming when she heard her name being called.

"Yeah, what's going on?" she asked, rising to the side of her cot.

"The first sergeant needs to see you." Another female from her unit spoke from the entrance of the tent.

Kacee felt sure she was being awakened to receive a message from one of her sisters. She'd been expecting the death of her mother since before the deployment. Her mother was deteriorating from a stroke and Alzheimer's in a nursing home in Louisiana.

Kacee's bunkmate, Alice, was also awakened and followed Kacee to the first sergeant's office. The captain and a chaplain were waiting for her, faces long and grim in the dim light.

The first sergeant pulled out a chair, "I think you should sit down."

Kacee studied his somber look. He had been a longtime friend. She'd known him most of her ten years with the Guard.

To break the cold silence, Kacee said, "If someone called about my mom, it's okay. I knew it was coming."

After a moment, the first sergeant seemed to know nothing else to do but blurt out the awful words: "Patrick's been killed."

Kacee felt she'd been hit in her belly with the butt end of a rifle. Her head began to pound as though all the oxygen was being sucked from the room. She could hear her heart beat in her ears, someone was holding a pillow tight against her face. She was fighting to breathe. She was frozen in a dark vault. She clutched the chair seat as tight as she could.

Everyone stared, waiting for her collapse. Only her tears had a will of their own.

"Are you sure?" she finally asked. "What happened?"

The first sergeant gave the information that had been received from the Red Cross. Shaking, but trying to remain composed, Kacee looked at Alice.

"I won't let this destroy me. He wouldn't want that."

Alice stooped next to Kacee and placed her arms around her shocked friend's shoulders. Kacee had often told her how Patrick was the first man she'd learned to trust and love since her divorce ten years before. "He's brought me so far," she said. "He taught me that I had to love myself before I could love anyone else. We were making plans for the future."

A doctor stood by to make sure Kacee would be okay and could get back to sleep.

"This is a dream," she finally said. "It has to be a dream. I have to call my sisters."

Alice helped Kacee make the call to Atlanta before leading her back to the tent. Lying down, Kacee knew she wouldn't be in Georgia for Patrick's memorial. Their not being married would prevent that. All she could do now was try and keep her sanity until May, when her unit returned to the states. Too often since August she had stood to honor fallen soldiers in Afghanistan as military vehicles took flag draped caskets across the airstrip, and soldiers placed them on a plane for the final trip home. Now when they rolled past, she would see only Patrick.

~ ELEVEN ~

"THANK YOU FOR CALLING. We'll see you then."

Deborah placed the receiver in its cradle. At the moment, the house was empty except for her and Dave. They had made it through Thursday with visits from friends after a phone chain had been created from one friend to another. Deborah knew how difficult it was for everyone to express sorrow. At times like these there were just no words in the language for expressions of condolence or the heartfelt gratitude that she and Dave felt for all the visits, phone calls, and hugs. In days to come she knew that without the love and prayers from so many, she and Dave would probably have never been able to reach for the sun that lay beneath the horrendous darkness encumbering their lives.

Now on Friday morning, a new person, their casualty assistance officer from Fort Benning, brought the second knock to the door. He brought with him a benefit check to help with initial expenses and informed Dave and Deborah of the anticipated date Patrick's body would arrive from Iraq. The process included an autopsy at the military hospital at Dover Air Force Base in Delaware, where Patrick would be dressed in full uniform for his arrival in Columbus. A soldier from the Second Armored Cavalry Regiment at Fort Polk would fly to Dover to escort Patrick home. An added delay came with Monday, February 16th, being a federal holiday.

Deborah also answered phone calls from out-of-state friends and news media from Georgia and California while Dave forced himself to eat and remain intact. After placing the phone in its cradle for the fifth time, Deborah looked at her husband who sat on the sofa, reading the local newspaper article about Patrick.

She couldn't believe how fast information had traveled over national news wires.

"That was Karon, Kacee's sister from Atlanta. She said that Kacee's CO is allowing her to come home. Their oldest sister, Kristin, is coming from Louisiana. They'll all be here by Wednesday."

"I'm glad to hear that," Dave said. "I'll just be glad to know when our boy'll be home."

"Me, too, honey." Deborah looked at her husband, feeling as helpless as if they'd been capsized into a raging sea and she could do nothing to pull him from the swells. But she had to remain strong, keep her own emotions intact. The next week would not get any easier.

On Tuesday night, following Thursday morning's notification, Deborah and Dave pulled into the parking lot at Striffler-Hamby Funeral Home. Before they arrived, a cameraman with Channel Four's news had already captured the flag-draped casket that had arrived at seven p.m. Inside the building they stood in front of another professional cavalry soldier in a small, dimly lit room with a sofa and a desk holding a lamp and flower arrangement. Soft, peaceful music wafted from the ceiling. Staff Sergeant Anderson, already a veteran of Iraq, stood professionally poised but sorrowful in his dress greens and black Stetson with the gold cord, a symbol worn proudly by the cavalry soldier. With despair in his eyes, he spoke with a steady, but empathetic voice.

"Sergeant Major and Mrs. Tainsh, on behalf of the United States Army Second Armored Cavalry Regiment, I am proud and honored to have been selected to bring your son back home to you. Although no words can soothe your loss, I want you to know that I stood watch, and guarded every move that was made to ensure that Sergeant Tainsh arrived home with honor. That all customs allotted to a fallen soldier were followed as he was carried to the plane before anyone else was allowed to board, and removed in the same manner."

Realizing Staff Sergeant Anderson's struggle to return a fallen comrade to his parents, Deborah and Dave held back their tears.

With all his years of active duty and service during war times, Dave knew firsthand the hardship on the living soldiers.

They extended their hands as Anderson presented gifts brought from the Second Armored Cavalry Regiment's Second Battalion, Eagle troop.

"On behalf of the unit I would like to present you with the cavalry Stetson, spurs, and saber, symbols of the United States Army cavalry scout."

What irony, Deborah thought, as Dave accepted the saber in its casing. She had discovered from a book that during the First Crusades the European soldiers had adopted the light cavalry and the saber's curved shape from the Muslim enemy. Now it seemed that the course of history had wafted to her door, bringing seeds of blood that had traveled from centuries past and over seven thousand miles to rest in her husband's hands.

After accepting the gifts, Deborah and Dave thanked the young man for all he had done for them and for his country. To ease the sergeant, Dave insisted he allow them to take him out for the biggest steak they could find. At the restaurant, they talked about his family. He had not been long returned from Iraq where he had experienced his own close calls. By the end of the evening, Dave and Deborah felt as though they had spent time with another son.

But the ensuing days came one behind the other, captured by an agonizing surreal reality. The two of them just knew the phone would ring any time and Patrick's voice would be on the other end, or that an e-mail message would pop up with, "Hey, just letting you know I'm okay." But those moments had ended with a flying piece of shrapnel from a man-made bomb on a road in Baghdad.

On Wednesday, Dave and Deborah received further help from Fort Benning's mortuary service representative. This time the visit to the house brought a review of all that the military provided for the service member's funeral. Then came the meeting with the funeral home to review all they would manage by way of communications with Ft. Benning's casualty assistance office. By afternoon, all arrangements were completed for having a memorial service with full military honors at the funeral home chapel on Friday afternoon. A memorial had been chosen to remember Patrick the way he left home: Standing on two strong feet, not lying prone in a flag draped box. The sight would have been more than they could bear, though Dave and Deborah still stood proud regarding the life their son had chosen, and they believed in their nation's call.

That evening, Dave sat in the family room with Jason watching the sports channel while Deborah sat at the kitchen table with Rose Hendrix, who had brought dinner.

"There's no need to feel guilty, Rose." Deborah looked at her friend, trying to comfort her. "There's a reason for everything. Be thankful that Christian is still alive and well."

"I know, but Dave didn't deserve this. He's had a hard enough life. I'm worried about him. Do you think he'll be okay?"

"He's strong, Rose. We'll get through this one way or the other. He's a survivor. You know that."

Deborah handed Rose another tissue and hugged her. "Just pray us through this. That's all that can be done. Whether we like it or not, it was Patrick's time. And as I told Dave the morning we were notified, we could have lost Patrick years ago under not-so-heroic circumstances. If we had to lose him, at least he was happy and doing something worthy that he loved."

"You're right," Rose said. "I guess I better say goodnight to the big guy. Call me if you need anything."

"We will. Tell Christian hello for us when you talk to him, and to stay safe."

On Friday morning Deborah stood alone on the back porch with her coffee, trying to prepare herself for the afternoon service. The trees scattered the land on the sides and back of the house with their February gray. An occasional squirrel stirred the crisp, dry leaves on the earth's floor. From the corner of her eye, she caught sight of a large wing. From the depths of the skeletal woodlands, a red-tailed hawk soared straight into the white oak, not fifty feet away. The two stared at one another. Deborah smiled through her tears, before turning to leave.

By 1:30 p.m., a misty rain and gray sky turned to pure azure. Entering the funeral home with Jason and Sindy, Deborah and Dave made their way toward the chapel. Kacee and her sisters followed. One of Dave's former young Marines had flown from North Carolina and walked beside his sergeant major.

"This makes me proud," Dave said. "Look how packed that room is."

Deborah stood amazed at the crowd entering from another door at the far end from them. The majority of people had never known Patrick. Not counting soldiers and officers who came from Fort Benning and Fort Polk, all the others were family, friends, and acquaintances that she and Dave had made or become reacquainted with since returning to Georgia. Former high school friends greeted Dave after having seen his name in the newspaper.

While Deborah stood in the greeting room next to the chapel, a woman she'd never met approached her.

"You don't know me," she said. "But I want you to know that I care. I'm retired Army."

With the sincerest smile, the stranger laid five white carnations in Deborah's hands. Deborah felt touched more than her simple words, "thank you," could express.

She felt, just as Dave did, that it was a great comfort to see so many there to honor and remember their son.

"I remember being spit on at the Los Angeles airport when I came home from Vietnam," Dave said. "It's good, now, to see support for the troops and the fallen. It's much needed and appreciated."

In the greeting room, Deborah saw guests gathered around a television. Away from Dave's sight, she shattered with tears against a friend's shoulder after seeing selected photos of Patrick move across the screen. She had chosen forty photos of Patrick at different ages that showed him living the way he loved. The first picture was one of him at less than a year old and in the arms of his birth mother. Others included frozen moments of him caught in perfect form riding a wave, lifting into the air or doing a handstand on a skateboard, snowboarding down Bear Mountain, or wearing camouflage in the training swamps at Fort Polk. There was the one from Christmas with Patrick, Sindy, and Jason grinning from ear to ear and wearing their matching shirts, the one of Kacee sitting in Patrick's lap.

And there was the last family photo that would ever be taken. While Patrick was home on his final Christmas, knowing he was deploying by March or April, Deborah had looked in the Yellow Pages for a professional photographer. She had known it would be difficult to locate someone who wasn't booked, or was willing to open business doors during Christmas holidays. The photographer who consented was retired Army and gladly opened his studio to take what would be her family's last formal sitting. Patrick stood in his Army dress greens next to his dad in his Marine Corps blues with Deborah and Jason on the opposite side.

Another special photo recorded Patrick when he was seventeen and with his best friend, Chris, a few days after Chris's high school graduation. Showing "thumbs up," Patrick leaned against the back panel of a white limo. Chris stood with his arms hanging over the top of the open limo door. They had known each other since age thirteen. From the vehicle's open sunroof, one end of a surfboard set slanted and protruding from inside the vehicle, pointed toward the sky. They were handsome blondes on their way to fly to Cape Hatteras, where Patrick's grandmother once lived and where he had surfed as a young boy.

Chris and his wife, Lisa, had flown from California for the service. Deborah asked them and Kacee to sit in the front family row. After the reverend opened the service, Chris walked to the podium with swollen eyes. Taking deep breaths, he read the eulogy he had written:

> I remember the day I met Patrick. We were on the
> school bus. Roughly 1984. We were in eighth grade. I
> remember he had a sticker on the collar of the windbreaker
> he was wearing. It read Thrasher. I knew about the
> magazine and that drew me to him to introduce myself, as I
> knew this was someone I wanted to know. He was a skater

and into skateboards like I was. And this was the beginning of a twenty-year relationship. I'm here today to tell you not about our relationship, but to give you insight into Patrick as a person. His story, to me, is really about a journey. One that is all about growth, adventure, experience, walking tall, falling hard, picking yourself up, and finally finding your calling and achieving goals.

Patrick was my best friend, brother, my surfing buddy, uncle to my unborn children. We never fought, and only rarely had harsh words for each other. He was the young boy who became a man who grew up through experience, and always sought out adventure. I can tell you about the tattoo on his wrist under his watch that stood for strength. He was strong. He endured the trials and tribulations of our teenage years in stride. Sometimes I don't know how he did it. He loved the ocean. The tattoo band on his arm represented his love for both coasts and that he had surfed on both. We were in the water a lot when we were younger. Up and down the coast of California. We surfed in Cape Hatteras in Carolina. We ran wild in Virginia Beach. Camped at Santa Barbara. We had lots of fun. Patrick was there when I needed a friend to talk to.

My family looked upon Patrick as the brother I never had, as we were always together. He and I had a very similar bond; we were only children and our fathers were career military men. We were brought up with manners and respect for others. Every holiday we always expected Patrick. To this day my mom keeps a plate for him at the dinner table every holiday, expecting him. He would always make an appearance. This is one of my fondest memories. Patrick and I never sought out things that would get us in trouble as kids. But we always managed to get into something. I remember teaching him to snowboard and the many trips that he and I went on. I remember him busting up his ankle on the slopes and having to ride in the back of a truck all the way down the mountain (some four hours) with three guys giving him grief. The significance of this is that he stayed strong and didn't whine about the pain or complain.

Patrick in his later years moved around a bit, doing it all. He was a gourmet chef. He could cook a meal from crumbs. I can tell you Patrick had a way about things. He needed to experience things first hand. Never was he afraid to leap into the unknown. Oh the stories I can tell you about him. But I won't do that here.

I want to tell you that Patrick was a good person with a good soul. He cared for people and knew the difference between right and wrong. His life was lived like the chapters of a book. Building upon the last and learning from the beginning. Patrick was a person on a journey that led him to his calling: the Army. He has made our families proud. We have been there through thick and thin and the one thing that stands as his legacy is that he went on this journey we call life, seeking adventure and new experiences while holding his head high. He had found his calling and there was honor in this new adventure. The structure and discipline that he found in his new life was something that Patrick relished, it was the enrichment that made him grow and blossom. He told me in one of our last conversations that he was eager to be part of something that makes a difference and that his new job was just what he needed. Patrick is home now and safe in our hearts. This journey has added another chapter to the book. His memory will live strong.

Peace lilies and various basket arrangements that had come from friends and strangers surrounded the chapel walls. Deborah saw the two large arrangements of mixed red, white, and blue fresh flowers she had ordered. One sat on each side of the table in front of the chapel. The cavalry Stetson, spurs, and saber were placed on the table with Patrick's photo. His Purple Heart and Bronze Star medals lay beside them in their cases. His Silver Star for being a selfless man, who had saved other lives the night he died, had not yet arrived. The day before the memorial, a phone call had come from Baghdad from Patrick's commanding officer, Captain Stacey Corn. With all the courage he had, the CO talked with both Deborah and Dave. He spoke his feelings about Patrick, the cavalryman. And also shared the dream he had the night Patrick died. With an e-mail from the captain that said the same, Deborah had arranged for a friend to read the words at the service.

Sergeant Major and Mrs. Tainsh. Below is what I wrote for the memorial service we had here in Baghdad. Once again I want to offer my deepest sympathies to you. I'll see you on the high ground.

The letter went on.

Sergeant Tainsh was one of the absolute best NCOs I have ever had the privilege to work with. Sergeant Tainsh had an excellent reputation throughout the Squadron. I knew about Sergeant Tainsh well before I came to Eagle Troop. It was a proud day for me when I was able to promote him to sergeant. I asked Sergeant Tainsh to be my gunner due to his discipline and consummate professionalism. I could not have found someone finer to be on my truck. He and I became very close due to all the time we spent together. I came to think of him as a brother. He was always there helping me out, sacrificing his personal time for me. There was nothing he wouldn't do for me nor I for him.

Sergeant Tainsh was always in a good mood and always worked to get me to smile when I was in a bad mood. He was constantly talking about his dad and his fiancée Kacee. He truly loved and admired his father and his biggest fear was to disappoint him.

Sergeant Tainsh was the best scout I have ever seen. He was constantly seeing things others would not. He was constantly working to be the best and would not accept mediocrity. After just about very patrol, Sergeant Tainsh would ask me what he could do better. Constantly seeking improvement. Sergeant Tainsh was absolutely amazing. There were several times that Sergeant Tainsh expertly maneuvered the Troop into the area we were operating by my just calling him and telling him we needed help.

On the night of 11 February, Sergeant Tainsh made the ultimate sacrifice for those around him. We spotted some men acting strange on the opposite side of a canal. We observed them for about five minutes. Sergeant Tainsh was constantly giving me spot reports pertaining to their actions. When the IED went off, Sergeant Tainsh was mortally wounded but immediately started laying down suppressive fire in order to secure the area for the medic to move forward. Sergeant Tainsh fired about 400 rounds and only stopped when he felt the area was secured. He then dropped down and tapped me on the shoulder to let me know he was wounded. What kind of man, who is mortally wounded, worries more about others around him than himself? He's called a hero.

Sergeant Tainsh, I will never forget you. You are my hero. Thank you for all that you did for me and your fellow soldiers. Sergeant Tainsh, I will always cherish the memories I have of you. You are what makes America great. I'll see you on the high ground.

After those words the captain had written:

The night of the attack I was having trouble sleeping due to the fact I was worried about Sergeant Tainsh. When I finally fell asleep, I had a dream and in that dream I was frantically searching for Sergeant Tainsh. I kept calling for him and couldn't find him anywhere. Finally I heard him say, "I'm over here, sir." I went around a corner and there was a real bright light. Sergeant Tainsh was standing there surrounded by this light. He was dressed in surfer shorts and a t-shirt with a backpack on. He smiled at me and said, "Here I am, sir. Don't worry about me. Everything's all right. I'm

*going to be fine." I smiled back at him and said O.K. He
turned and threw up his hand and waved good bye and
walked off into the light. Ever since then I have had a sense of
peace and well being about him. I know for a fact he is in a
better place.*

After the letter was read, Deborah's friend Christine approached
the podium and sang "Battle Hymn of the Republic" a cappella.
Deborah knew from studying poetry that Julia Ward Howe had
written the words as a poem during the Civil War. She believed it
fitting for Patrick's service.

Outside the rear chapel doors that were opened to the back
parking lot, six Army riflemen stood in formation. The first round
of gunfire caused Deborah to jump in her seat. She squeezed Dave's
hand as silent tears eased down her face. Her husband remained
as stoic and still as the stone Marines on the Iwo Jima memorial.
"Taps" wafted through the chapel like an invisible saber, piercing
hearts to their greatest depth, releasing tears of the staunchest.
General Freakley from Fort Benning walked toward Dave and
faced him with a folded flag that held an empty shell casing. On
bended knee, he presented the emblem to Dave with a message
of condolence and gratitude for Patrick's service. Dave nodded
and said thank you as the general stood and saluted.

After the closing prayer, Deborah, Dave, and their family
followed the reverend from the chapel to the sound of the organist
playing "Onward Christian Soldiers."

Later in the evening Deborah said to Dave, "Everyone knew
Patrick the boy, the man, and hero. And I know that Patrick was
proud of you today. You looked like you were still ready to lead a
unit in those dress blues."

"I wore them to honor Patrick," was his only reply.

After all the guests left, they both agreed that with the
exception of Patrick's uncle from North Carolina arriving
inebriated after the service had begun, and his cousin's cell phone
ringing during the reverend's opening prayer, it had been a flawless,
beautiful service. Dave managed a joke. "If the reverend hadn't

been praying," he said, "I would've stood and announced for somebody to please answer the damn phone. It might be Patrick calling!" In the pain they laughed for a single moment, knowing that Patrick would be grinning and saying, "Hey man, it ain't no big deal. And anyway, what's all the hoopla for? I was just doin' my job."

~ TWELVE ~

AT THE TAINSH HOME, Kacee stood in a haze in the room Patrick and she had shared during the 2002 Christmas holidays. For the first time, she noticed the 1936 Norman Rockwell print that hung on the wall. From the forlorn appearance in their lowered eyes and sad faces, the solemn young couple whose heads leaned against one another seemed to grieve with her.

The memorial service was done and guests had left the house. Her sisters had returned to their hotel. With jet lag added to the emotional wipeout, she was ready to sleep for days. She lifted her travel bag to the bed. On top of everything lay Patrick's t-shirt. It was the one she kept beneath her pillow in Afghanistan. She pulled it out and held it close. *Second ACR Eagle Troop* was written across the back above two curved, crossed sabers. She had not washed it since Patrick took it off and handed it to her. It held his smell, his sweat, and his skin particles. It was all she had left of him. He had given it to her the last weekend they spent together in New Orleans.

In February, Patrick had driven the four hours from Fort Polk to Covington to pick her up for the one hour drive to the Big Easy. They wandered through museums and sipped mint juleps at the Maison Bourbon Jazz Club. They sat at Pat O'Brien's outdoor garden cafe and shared shrimp creole.

Kacee remembered her mother's love for Mardi Gras, how she would take Kacee and her sisters, when they were young, to watch the annual crazy celebration. Now she had her memories of walking with Patrick down Decatur Street to Café Du Monde for coffee and beignets, listening to him tell her that Jackson Square, the heart of the French Quarter, was used in the early days to train, drill, and parade military troops. She had listened intently when he told her about Baroness Micaela Almonester de Pontalba, who had all the Pontalba buildings constructed around the square. Patrick had told her that in 1855 Clark Mills created the square's famous statue of Andrew Jackson tipping his hat from the back of his rearing horse.

"The statue is to honor the hero of the Battle of New Orleans in 1815," he said, "but it's also said that the tip of the hat was to show respect to the baroness who once lived in the mansion that Jackson faces."

Laying the t-shirt on the bed, Kacee thought, *that's my man, my hero, and gentleman.*

She would wrap herself forever with those memories. They would be frozen in time like the white-faced mime they had watched on St. Anne's Street. A tall, slender figure in white top hat, tails, and shoes frozen in the motion of taking a single step, one foot in front of the other, one hand holding a stiff leash attached to an invisible dog, and the other touching the top of his hat as though the wind were attempting to blow it away. She would never let go of the feeling of the soft breeze as they walked hand-in-hand past the quaint shops along the sidewalks, listened to the sound of bells pealing from the St. Louis Cathedral. She knew Patrick would not want her to grieve, to cry forever, but she asked him to forgive the tears now stinging her eyes. She looked at Patrick's photo, the one where he stood in a circle of five Iraqi children, his hands on their heads.

"I miss you," she said, "but I'm going to be okay, I promise. I know you'd want that." She placed a kiss on her index finger, and pressed it against Patrick's face. From beneath his helmet, sunglasses, and flak jacket he smiled back at her.

Patrick had believed he was making a contribution toward a better life and future for Iraqi children. In letters he had written to her, Dave, and Deborah, he talked about how he couldn't believe the poverty that "the monster" Saddam had caused his own people. How it broke his heart not to have food or water to give the begging children. How filthy the streets of Baghdad were. How, closer to the end of his year, he was tired of the hellhole, ready to come home. With Patrick's shirt against her skin, she shut off the light and lay down beneath the sheets. Pulling herself into a fetal position, she made as much of herself as possible be in contact with what she had left to hold onto. Saying goodnight to Patrick, she fell asleep with tears sliding to her pillow.

On Saturday morning, Dave stirred in the kitchen by six a.m., ready for coffee and a cigarette. "Damn," he said, when the cup he pulled from the cabinet slipped from his hand. He pulled the trashcan from under the sink and held it to the counter, then raked in the broken pieces.

From the guestroom next to the kitchen, Kacee awakened at the sound of the crashing cup. She lay still, thinking she was dreaming until she heard the garage door open. She figured it was Dave, up and about. Lying beneath the down comforter, she thought how she had come to love this place as her second home. She had told her best friends how lucky she was to have become a part of the Tainsh family, how they would make great in-laws. Her sisters had been happy that she had bonded so quickly with Patrick's parents. She'd been running from one relationship to the other since her divorce. Now Dave had become the dad she hadn't had since she was ten. With her mother teetering on the brink of death, Deborah had become special, too. Now she feared that with the loss of Patrick she would lose them. With the memorial service over and the guests gone, she wanted to spend time with them before returning to Afghanistan.

Hearing Dave return to the kitchen, Kacee decided to see if he was okay.

"Good morning," she said, walking into the aroma of coffee.

"And to you, too," Dave said, smiling. "Did you get any sleep?"

"Not too much. I cried most of the night."

Kacee welcomed Dave's hug when he placed his arms around her shoulders.

"Thanks, I need that," she said. "You got an extra cup?"

"Here you go," he said. "I'll try not to break this one. Sorry I woke you."

"I was already awake, just thinking." Kacee smiled, holding her cup up as Dave poured the coffee with a quivering hand.

"Hey, you two, save some for me." Deborah had heard the cup shatter from the back of the house.

"What are you doing up so early?" Dave asked.

"Oh, I just couldn't sleep this morning."

Deborah returned Dave's morning kiss and Kacee's hug. With their cups full, they settled in the family room. A small wreath of dried eucalyptus and simple flowers with a red, white, and blue ribbon with stars set on the mantle of the rock fireplace.

"That's pretty," Kacee said. "Where'd that come from?"

"Old acquaintances in California." Deborah said. "They saw Patrick's picture on the San Diego news and contacted us. It's amazing how folks come out of the woodwork in a crisis."

"That's so true," Kacee said, taking a sip of coffee. "I was shocked when my CO arranged for me to come from Afghanistan. He didn't have to do that."

"Well, doors open where they're suppose to, along with the closings," Deborah said as she raked her hands through disheveled hair. "When do you have to be back at Bagram?"

"In two weeks. I'm driving back to Louisiana with Kristin tomorrow. I need to see Mom. Then I'll go back to Atlanta for my flight out."

"By the way," Deborah said. "How is your Mom? I haven't even had time to talk to you about her."

"Actually, she's at hospice care now. I thought it was Mom they were going to tell me about instead of Patrick."

"Bless your heart, honey. I know you've got to be at your wit's end right now."

Sitting in the chair at the corner of the sofa, Kacee pulled her knees to her chest as she sipped the coffee. Dave stepped outside while the women talked.

Kacee told Deborah that her father had died when he was only fifty, and that her mother, a nurse who never remarried, was now sixty-nine. She had suffered a stroke several years earlier. Alzheimer's followed.

"She's so young," Deborah said, from her corner on the sofa. "I'm so sorry. I certainly admire you. I can't even begin to comprehend the burden you're carrying right now. You just take care of yourself. I know all this is so hard. I wish you didn't have to go back to Afghanistan."

Before Kacee spoke again, the phone rang. Deborah answered, hoping it wasn't someone asking for Dave. He still couldn't talk without losing his composure. She knew he didn't want anyone, not even her, to see him break down. But whether he realized it or not, she knew he had cried alone in the bathroom from the day the notification came. With his iron will, he had remained stoic in the receiving line at the chapel and afterward at the house. But that was his way. He could put the face on that he needed for the world outside his private domain. It was what she knew she would endure later, alone with him, that she worried about.

Jason was on the phone. "It's just me. I'm checking to make sure you guys are okay."

"We're good for now."

"Okay," he said. "Tell Kacee we'll see her before she leaves. Call if you or Dave need anything."

Over the past week, Jason and Sindy had been extra strength for Deborah and Dave, constantly reminding them how much Patrick loved what he did and what he had always said: "I'm doin' my job and I love it. Don't worry about me."

But Deborah's greatest fear would linger for days, even months: Where would her husband's mind lead him? Losing Patrick was like draining Dave's own blood. He thrived when Patrick thrived. Otherwise, he walked around half a person. Deborah wondered how her marriage would be affected by her stepson's death, whether or not Dave would distance himself as days passed, how he would ultimately deal with the loss of his only child, his heart and soul. After difficult years, he and Patrick had finally become best friends.

Deborah knew that Dave's biggest question was why God had taken Patrick just as his life had finally grown so promising. But her husband was not one to talk about things that bothered him;

he kept most things in his head. He never spoke much about God or faith and never allowed an open door for discussion with her. She had never been sure if he couldn't or wouldn't. All he ever alluded to over the years was that there were no atheists in foxholes. After Patrick's death, the only thing he had said about God was that God had let him down.

"I prayed every day, two and three times a day and every night," he had said. "He didn't answer my prayers, and I'm angry. Why did he have to take my son right when everything was going so good for him?"

Deborah was not able to answer these questions. All she could do was remind Dave that prayers had not been answered for many families who had lost a child. Not only those fighting in Iraq and Afghanistan, but those lost every day in unexpected ways, in the blink of an eye. On the morning they were notified about Patrick, Deborah wrapped her arms around her husband's neck, hugged him as tight as she could.

"I can't tell you how to feel, or how to get through this," she said. "I can only tell you that you have lost Patrick in a most honorable way. You have to remember that there was a time in his life when you could have lost him and you would have never forgiven yourself. You would have blamed yourself. Now, you have nothing to blame anyone for. Patrick chose something good. He lost his life doing good."

After Jason's call, Deborah answered a knock at the door. Kacee's sisters had returned from their hotel. Everyone from Miami, North Carolina, and California was headed back home. While Dave watched television, Deborah sat with Kacee and her sisters around the breakfast table. The sun fell through the bay windows. With the laptop on the table, they looked at the photos of Patrick that the funeral home had placed on a disc. The music that played behind the pictures only enhanced their silent tears.

"He was a walking miracle," Deborah said, watching the photos roll by.

Kacee wondered what Deborah was referring to. Then something came to mind that Patrick had written to her from

Iraq. He had once said he needed to tell her about ghosts from his past after they both returned home. But this wasn't the time to mention it.

"I'm so glad we got to see one another in Qatar," Kacee said. "We didn't think we'd ever get the trip coordinated. Our first sergeants finally helped make everything happen. Patrick arrived in Qatar on October fifth and I got there the night of the sixth."

"I'm just so glad it worked out for you both," Deborah said, knowing that Patrick had chosen to take his leave with Kacee rather than come home.

Kacee told Deborah and her sisters about the trip she'd made to see Patrick at Camp As Sayliyah. "You wouldn't believe what we did for privacy for three days and nights!" Kacee said, recalling her bittersweet memories. "We slipped past a guard and went inside a bunker that was surrounded by concrete, sandbags, and rocks. I'll never forget our last night together."

"It was meant to be and I'm glad that you can talk about him," Deborah said, wiping tears from her eyes.

On Sunday, after hugging Kacee and her sisters goodbye, Deborah and Dave packed for a trip to Fort Polk. The unit regiment had scheduled another memorial service. On Ash Wednesday, Deborah and Dave entered the post's main chapel. They knew the service was going to honor not only Patrick, but also PFC Ramirez, age nineteen, killed during the same ambush.

Before the service, they followed a lieutenant down a hallway, past chapel offices to a private room. Inside, PFC Ramirez's family waited. After the lieutenant introduced the families, Deborah handed Ramirez's mother a rose and gave her condolences with a hug. Then she listened to the grieving, but steady, woman as she spoke.

"I prayed with my rosary three times a day. I asked God to send my son home safe," she said.

"I know," Deborah responded. "We all prayed. Now we pray to get through it, and one day, understand."

The grieving mother smiled. "Yes, someday we will know," she said.

Deborah turned back to Dave to shake hands and receive condolences from a line that included unit wives and men Patrick and PFC Ramirez had served with. Some of the men had returned earlier from Iraq with wounds. Deborah would never forget the young soldier who spoke from the podium in the chapel, his right arm shattered by gunfire, still in a cast and sling. He forced back tears with a cracking voice as he read the words he had written to honor Patrick. All Deborah could think of was how much every American owed to those brave enough to help protect the American way of life. Although grieved, she and Dave still stood proud. Patrick's life was not lost without reason. *Kids killed in drive-by shootings and drugs—that was in vain,* she thought.

Dave's stoic gratefulness to others continued, but Deborah could hardly bear the pain in her husband's pale, sunken face. He had visibly aged over the past two weeks. With her arm wrapped in Dave's, Deborah walked to her seat at the front of the chapel, struggling to fight back tears and nausea as they passed the customary two rifles. Each one braced and balanced on its butt end, holding a helmet and dog tags with a pair of desert boots sitting at the foot. Photos of Patrick and PFC Ramirez sat between them. Following the chaplain's words, a sergeant major in Scottish kilt played "Amazing Grace" on bagpipes. Deborah wondered if he knew that Patrick was of Scottish heritage. When the service ended, Deborah walked again next to her husband to the front of the chapel. She picked up Patrick's photo. It was all that remained to take home.

~ THIRTEEN ~

IT WAS MID-MARCH. A ringing phone cancelled Dave's thoughts about reading the daily paper. After the call, he walked to the back porch and took a seat across from his wife.

"Hey beautiful, what 'cha thinking about?"

"I was thinking about how strong oaks are and the hawk that shows up now and then. Wondering if we'll see it again." Although she had pointed the large bird out to Dave, she had not shared the Indian myth with him. He was not ready to hear anything beyond his own reality. What had happened had happened. She knew her husband well enough to know he was living with an overwhelming loss. Nothing now was going to soothe him, especially a myth.

"Did I hear the phone ring?" She finally asked.

"Yeah. It was Lt. Johnson from Fort Polk. He says Patrick's personal items from the barracks and his car should be here next week."

"Does anyone have any idea when his stuff will come in from Iraq?" Deborah wanted to make sure the digital camera and portable DVD player that were mailed to Patrick for Christmas were returned. Swallowing the last drink from her coffee cup, she watched Dave light another cigarette. She thought how Christmas would certainly never be the same. The ten-foot Christmas tree that Dave had taken down the day the chaplain came now lay in its box in the garage, still waiting to reach the attic. If it ever got there, it may never come down again.

No, she thought to herself, still listening to Dave, *no future Christmas, nor day, would ever be the same.*

Even if the cannon blast of Patrick's death did not destroy her and Dave's renewed marriage, it had blown out a vital part of their life together, removing dreams for the future, one of the most difficult being no grandchildren from Tainsh blood. The big house in the trees surrounded by places to play hide and seek and a lake for fishing no longer had the same meaning as it did two years ago. It had taken Deborah years and leaving him to convince Dave to return to a calm life in Georgia, to retire in their dream home. But now, part of the dream was gone.

Dave finished another cigarette and spoke to Deborah again about Patrick's possessions that were still in Iraq.

"It's probably going to be a few months before anything else gets here from Baghdad," he said. "But that's normal. At least they sent his wallet, watch, and some photos back already."

Deborah set her coffee cup on the table beside her. Dave remained in the chair across the way. The morning sun was moving higher above the house.

"I hope the Camry's in good shape after being in storage for a year," Deborah said.

"The lieutenant said it had a flat tire that's been fixed, and a crack in the windshield. It was sitting outside all this time. So the crack probably came from the mix of hot and cold weather. I'll have it all repaired after it gets here." Dave took a drag from another cigarette and blew the smoke away from Deborah's face.

"So what are your plans today?" he asked.

"I think I'll begin putting the stuff away that's still in the dining room. That's why I bought the trunk that's at the foot of the bed. I'm storing all the cards, correspondence, and news articles in it."

Dave rose from the chair and kissed his wife on the side of the face. "Well, I think I'll go to the garden shop. I need to get this yard in order."

Deborah was glad to hear that her husband was going out for a while. She didn't care the reason. As long as he wasn't sitting on the sofa from sunup until he fell asleep with Fox News. Some days it was more than she could stand to watch. In her view, his total retirement wasn't good for him now. His only hobbies were yard work, cleaning the bathrooms, reading the daily newspaper, watching the news, and smoking. Patrick had warned him about that over the years. He had told him more than once that he needed a serious hobby like fishing, golfing, or something. Now Deborah would have to remind him.

Deborah sat for a few more minutes. She watched several squirrels chase one another around the oak in front of the deck, challenging each other for seed in the feeder. *Probably the highlight of their day,* she thought, *with not a worry about a single thing.* A line in a poem came to mind that she couldn't remember verbatim, but its essence had remained with her: simple animals lived to live, never knowing to worry or grieve over death or dying.

Watching the playful squirrels she wondered who had it better, them or humans.

In the kitchen, she set her cup in the sink. With a bottle of water from the cabinet, she shuffled to the dining room in her sock feet. Cards, letters, correspondence, and other items covered the long table. They had been there for nearly a month, waiting for her to bring a sense of organization back to the room, back to their lives.

The stacks of envelopes brought a sense of peace. They showed how so many had made known their care and compassion. Even people they didn't know had sent cards from various cities and states through the Department of the Army or by contacting newspaper offices that had run articles about Patrick. She pulled a chair from the end of the table and took a seat. She picked up one envelope at a time and reviewed the names in the left hand corners. One that had been particularly meaningful to her and Dave had come from a man in Atlanta. He had mailed his letter in care of the regiment at Fort Polk, Louisiana. Deborah opened the envelope and read again:

> *Dear Friend:*
> *You may be interested in the enclosed passage, which was read at the memorial service for retired Lieutenant General M. Collier Ross of the United States Army last year in Atlanta. I found it a moving and encouraging piece and hope that you might as well.*

Collier was a devoted friend to—as well as a leader of— his troops during his many years of service to our country. Beginning life as a country boy in Missouri, he went on to become Senator Harry Truman's last appointee to West Point. He eventually became the first graduate after WWI to command every type of military unit, from platoon to the largest standing army in world history. He served in two wars and was twice wounded in combat.

If he were here and had the opportunity, I know General Ross would tell you himself of his admiration of you and yours and his gratitude for your sacrifice. I pass this text along to you as a tribute to your brave fallen one and in memory of an outstanding friend of every American defender, General Collier Ross.

It is a small thing, I know. With it comes my sincere best wishes and kindest regards.

Very truly yours,
Jack Lawson

Deborah placed the letter on the table and began reading the text that had accompanied it. It read:

Death is nothing at all. I have only slipped away into the next room. I am I, and you are you. Whatever we were to each other, that we are still. Call me by my old familiar name; speak to me in the easy way which you always used. Put no difference in your tone; wear no forced air of solemnity or sorrow. Laugh as we always laughed at the little jokes we enjoyed together. Play, smile, think of me, pray for me. Let my name be ever the household word that it always was. Let it be spoken without effort, without the trace of a shadow on it. Life means all that it ever meant. It is the same as it ever was; there is unbroken continuity. Why should I be out of mind because I am out of sight? I am waiting for you, for an interval, somewhere very near, just around the corner. All is well.

—Henry Scott Holland, 1847-1918

Deborah wiped the tears from her cheeks. She had responded by sending an e-mail message to Jack Lawson, thanking him for his tribute and thoughtfulness. It was these kindnesses from so many that kept her and Dave going.

She placed the pages back inside the brown envelope they had arrived in and laid it on the corner of the table with white envelopes full of condolences. In another stack she placed everything that had come from military brass, congressman, senators, governors, and the White House, including letters from Donald Rumsfeld, the secretary of defense, and President Bush. Because they had lived in California for so many years, where Patrick had enlisted, they had received a letter from Governor Arnold Schwarzenegger with his original signature.

What a price, Deborah thought. *You see that Patrick? I can't believe what you'd do for attention from another movie star turned governor. And here's the one signed by President Bush. And look at this, he's addressing your dad on a first name basis.*

Deborah read the letter addressed to Sergeant Major David Tainsh, USMC, Ret.

> *Dear David:*
> *I am deeply saddened by the loss of your son, Sergeant Patrick Tainsh, USA.*
> *Patrick's noble service in Operation Iraqi Freedom has helped to preserve the security of our homeland and the freedoms America holds dear. Our Nation will not forget Patrick's sacrifice and unselfish dedication in our efforts to make the world more peaceful and more free. We will forever honor his memory. Laura and I send our heartfelt sympathy. We hope you will be comforted by your faith and the love and support of your family and friends. May God bless you.*
> *Sincerely,*
> *George W. Bush*

After reading it through, Deborah placed the letter back in the large brown envelope with the return address that said The

White House, Washington DC 20502 and placed it by itself. Dave was proud of that letter and wanted to frame it. Going through more and more envelopes, she came across a letter that was more special to her than the one from the president, written by someone who had served with Patrick.

> *Dear Sergeant Major Tainsh and Mrs. Tainsh:*
> *My deepest condolences go out from my family to yours. We are very sorry and sad. Your son was a great man. I am sure you are very proud of him. I certainly am. I was privileged to know him and serve with him in the Second Squadron, Second Armored Cavalry Regiment. I served as squadron commander from June 2001 to July 2003.*
>
> *I had the good fortune to meet your son early in my tour with the Second Squadron and watch your son grow and interact with his many friends and unit, Eagle Troop. I also got to know him personally because he always seemed to be in the right place at the right time both on duty and off. I often sought out his opinion on how things were going for the troopers from his perspective. We had long talks about training and quality of life for soldiers in the barracks. He was always honest, thoughtful, and articulate and had a good sense of humor. I enjoyed every opinion he declared and every conversation we had. He gave me great advice that I put to action in order to make our unit better.*
>
> *After talking with Specialist, then Corporal, then Sergeant Tainsh, my day was always better whether it was the motor pool at Fort Polk or in Baghdad. He had a positive attitude about everything. I counted on him, trusted him and loved him. I remember the sadness I had when I said goodbye to him in July. He was like a family member to me. A brother in arms. Your son was an expert cavalryman. I watched him operate, train, and perform many skills required by scouts. He was a true professional. He had a strong work ethic. He was a leader. Men followed him naturally. He was absolutely technically and tactically competent. He is a hero.*

My heart goes out to your family. I am very sorry. I will remember him forever.
Sincerely,
JR Armstrong, Lieutenant Colonel, Cavalry, US Army

Deborah smiled. "You made it, didn't you?" she said out loud. "I guess you're beaming at all of us." Deborah believed from the deepest chambers of her heart that those who went before their loved ones existed everywhere. She knew she couldn't reach out and touch her bonus son, but that he was still near. This was her peace of mind. If only she and Dave could talk together to comfort one another. But Dave kept his thoughts to himself and wasn't much on spiritual discussions. She knew he harbored too much anger right now. She expected him to blow any day. That's how it had always happened when he was stressed. He would be able to go only so long smoking and staring at the television while a volcano built inside him. With just the wrong word from her on an unexpected day and moment, an eruption would occur. She knew that sooner or later the loss of Patrick would bring out Dave's worst side. He had been controlled so far. Better than she had expected. But she was sure he'd rather be out in the yard screaming and ripping trees out of the ground. He had let her see only a few slight tears and a shaky lip once or twice.

After all the envelopes were organized, Deborah placed them in separate stacks and marked them. The obituary announcements for the Friday, February 20th at two p.m. memorial and leftover thank you cards were the last to be put away. She had already sent notes of appreciation to everyone who sent flowers and food.

She picked up the cassette created by the funeral home and the CD from the chapel at Fort Polk. She placed them in the special cloth-covered box she had purchased to hold all the memorial items. She added all the various envelopes and items, including a small book of poems that an unknown woman brought in person to their home. With the lid closed, she carried the box to the bedroom. She set it inside the dark brown trunk covered with old world maps she had bought and placed at the foot of their bed.

From the bedroom, Deborah heard Dave open the back door. She shut the trunk lid and spread a burgundy throw across the top. Walking down the hall to the kitchen, she knew Dave would be ready for lunch.

"Hey, what'd you get?" she asked.

"I ordered twelve azaleas from the lawn and garden shop. They're going to deliver them later today. Then I looked around for some wood to build the swing trellis you wanted. Have you checked e-mails this morning?"

Deborah walked to the end of the table where the laptop sat. "Doing it right now," she said.

Dave placed a gallon of milk and sandwich turkey in the refrigerator while Deborah signed into the e-mail. It had been their primary source of communication with Patrick during his time in Iraq. He had written only four or five letters that he mailed home. After that it was e-mail at least every two days to let everyone know he was okay. He also sent messages for things he needed, like the new pair of desert boots that Dave had ordered. Deborah hid them in a closet the day they appeared on the doorstep, the same day as the notification officer.

Closing the refrigerator door, Dave walked next to his wife. "Did we get anything?"

"Yep, here's a note from Kacee." They both read the message from Afghanistan.

Hey! How are y'all doing? I have been quite busy since I've been back. Instead of covering my work while I was gone, they let all the UCMJ actions pile up. Fortunately, it does keep me busy and it helps to keep my mind off things.

I just want you to know that Patrick brought a lot of nice things not only into my life, but my family's as well. My sisters said that after hearing everyone talk about how Patrick turned his whole life around for the better, it gave them inspiration to achieve more in their lives. Also, I just thought you should know that Patrick was one of the main reasons why I got Teacher of the Year. His positive attitude toward his

own profession was so "catchy" that it made me strive harder at my job. Also, anytime I was feeling discouraged he would give me motivating advice to follow.
I love y'all...take care...Kacee

A week later, an Atlas Van Lines truck arrived with Patrick's 1998 Camry and four large boxes of belongings. Dave greeted the driver at the top of the hill above the driveway. He watched the man drive the car from inside the trailer, down the driveway. With a dolly, the driver brought the boxes to the garage and placed them against the wall next to the back door. After the man left, Dave lit a cigarette, and stood staring at the stacked boxes. He couldn't grasp, did not want to accept, that these boxes, a car, and some military medals were all he had left of his son. Hearing Deborah open the door from the hall into the garage, he blinked back the tears.

"It's here," he said, blowing a puff of smoke towards space outside the garage. "But I can't go through it right now."

"Nobody's asking you to, honey." Deborah stepped beside him and placed her arm around his waist.

From the thick foliage on the other side of Patrick's car, a wild turkey made a guttural noise. The U.S. flag on the side of the garage moved slightly in the morning's easy breeze.

Dave threw his spent cigarette to the ground. "I need to look at the damage to the car."

Deborah followed him to the dusty emerald green Camry. Dave examined the crack in the windshield. It ran at an angle from the driver's side to the center. He opened the hood and checked the oil before taking a seat to turn the engine. The ignition and trunk key were still attached to a silver key ring with the round black inset, designed with the lightening bolt and *AC DC* lettering that represented the rock group. He ran the engine for a moment, then walked to the rear and opened the trunk. Inside were running shoes, extra boots, a bag of dirty clothes, and three books from history classes that Patrick was taking before orders for Iraq.

Deborah stood next to her husband, holding back tears, as she watched him move his hand across each item.

"Do you want me to take any of this into the garage?" she asked.

"You might want these." Dave handed the books to his wife. He knew how she was about books and history. She and Patrick could spend hours watching the History Channel, reading history books, discussing things. "I'll bring in the dirty clothes," he said.

Deborah took the books from her husband and turned toward the garage. Her chest felt filled with the weight of lead. She knew Dave was carrying a pack so heavy that he was moving from point A to point B by sheer force, and she could do nothing to ease his incomprehensible load.

~ FOURTEEN ~

DEBORAH WAS DRESSED and standing in front of the bathroom mirror, brushing her hair. After putting on a baseball cap, she walked to the garage. Dave was smoking, staring into the trees outside the open door.

"Honey, I'm going to the grocery store. Is there anything special you want?" she asked.

Dave did not look at her, but spoke in a low monotone.

"You can't get me what I want," he said. "I've lost everything. I don't have a damn reason to go on living. You don't know what it's like to lose a child. You still have Jason. I have no one."

Deborah had known that sooner or later these statements would rise like a boil to the tip of her husband's tongue. She had thought she would be prepared, but a storm surge felt like it was on the way as she spoke a single thought.

"I figured you'd get around to saying that."

To keep from screaming, she walked back to the kitchen. Acid burned in the pit of her stomach. All she could think of was how, over twenty years of marriage, she and Dave had suffered with one another through arguments of every kind, including disciplining Patrick when he was at his worst. Now with Patrick's death, another abyss was about to form. Old memories floated back up with burning reflux. Before their marriage they had talked about having children. But it was after Patrick came to live with them that Dave had changed his mind, adamant that he didn't want any more kids.

"I've got mine and you've got yours," he had said. "We don't need any." Deborah knew that part of her had died that day, along with the dream of having another baby. His voice burned as much today as it had all those years ago.

She had hoped they would never again be at this point. Certain wounds had healed over the years and through the separation. Dave had always been a good man and provider. He would kill for her. But issues involving a child were always different. Here she stood alive, and Jason was alive, while the child her husband adored was dead. She felt as empty and drained as a deep, dry well. She was trying to carry this final burden for her husband but now it seemed another gap was growing. And without divine intervention, which she wasn't so sure of anymore, the cut that lay wide open, bleeding in her heart, would fester and poison all they'd worked toward over the past two years.

Dave entered the kitchen and poured another cup of coffee. Deborah looked at him. Through the tears and anger she said as calmly as possible:

"I know you don't think I feel this loss as strong as you. He was your birth son. I was only the stepmom. But I was the mom who tried to help make a difference in his life. I worried while he was out late at night. I waited on the sidewalk and on the sofa. I wasn't perfect by any means. But I cared about what he was doing with his life. I did all I could to help both of you before he left home. And after all he overcame, I couldn't be prouder of him or in more pain than if he were my birth child. I've done everything I know to help you through this. And now you insinuate that *I'm* not worth living for! And as far as Jason goes, do you want me to tell him not to come around any more?"

Dave simply turned and walked away. His expression and the words from twenty years ago came back to Deborah. It was another time of not being able to deal with situations concerning Patrick. Even then he had looked at her with a cold expression that sent an alarm to her heart, saying, "No one, no one, will come between me and my son or before my son. Just leave me alone." Today, he didn't have to say it. She read it in his eyes, in the way he turned away.

Alone in the kitchen, Deborah cried. She wanted to believe in her heart that Dave had not meant what he said and what his body language conveyed. But the reality was like being scourged to the core of the heart.

In the days that followed, she was at a loss for what to do or say. She either went to the library or remained in the back of the house reading, while Dave drove around town or saturated himself with Fox News. It seemed that the house walls were cold and nervous, and any happiness had fled to hide in the mass of trees surrounding the yard, afraid to reappear. In her own anger, Deborah was not sure what good praying would even do. But someone, somewhere, who believed must have been praying for her. After a week of cold-stone silence in the house, Deborah felt she was sent a message. And it came from a complete stranger.

A friend had directed Deborah to a nonprofit group and a woman named Jane Langston to inquire about raising funds for children's books to provide to local children in Patrick's memory. Deborah and Dave had agreed earlier that doing something for others would give them a focus to ease the pain and carry on their son's name.

When Deborah called to arrange a meeting, a week after she and Dave had gone into silence, Jane spoke with the gentle voice Deborah so needed. After Deborah introduced herself over the phone, Jane told her she had heard about Patrick. She had been thinking about their loss. Deborah felt comforted when Jane shared that she and her husband had lost their only son four years before in a car accident.

"We know what you're going through," she said.

Deborah couldn't believe a total stranger was sharing her personal tragedy. The two women talked over the phone a while before meeting in person the next day.

When they met, it was as kindred spirits, not strangers. When Deborah walked through Jane's office door, the tears piled up in both their eyes.

"It's so good to meet you," Jane said with the warmest, most sincere smile that Deborah could have asked for, at a time she needed it most. "Please sit down."

Deborah felt comforted in the presence of this petite, attractive woman with the gentle face. Feeling comfortable, she proceeded to ask Jane if she could talk to her on a personal basis.

"I feel I'm here for you. Ask whatever you'd like," Jane said, looking at Deborah and smiling.

"Well, I know that you've already shared with me that the loss of your son has been very hard on both you and your husband. That your husband still can't talk about him."

"Yes, my husband keeps things to himself. Men just don't seem to be able to deal with situations the way we women do."

Deborah felt at ease and shared with Jane what Dave had said, and how devastated she was, though she wasn't totally surprised.

Leaving Jane Langston's office that day, Deborah realized she was not alone in her abysmal reality. Jane and her husband had experienced similar confrontations. Her husband would not speak of God or faith, and would no longer enter the doors of a church. She and Jane cried together, agreeing that no matter what, they knew their husbands loved them and didn't mean to cause them more pain. Faith would have to be the balm that brought eventual healing. And God's shoulders were certainly big enough to carry the anger that still welled up inside them all.

Deborah drove straight home. Walking to the back porch where Dave stood gazing into the woods, she went to him. Without a word, she hugged and kissed him, then walked inside the house. He needed time.

Later that evening, Dave listened as Deborah shared the story about Jane Langston and her husband's loss. Their son was only twenty-two. He had been a fireman who died in a freak car accident that not even the Ford Motor Company could resolve. The gas pedal on his car had stuck, causing Lance to be careened into a light pole and put in a coma from head injuries. He died a number of months later, in a nursing home.

"We're not the only ones suffering," Deborah said to her husband, again. "We're not alone." Without a word, Dave moved from his chair, pulled Deborah close and hugged her.

It's a beginning, Deborah thought to herself. *Thank you, God, it's a beginning.*

~ FIFTEEN ~

IT WAS THE SECOND week of June. Deborah and Dave sat in Covington, Louisiana, at Felding's Funeral Home. Three rows in front of them Kacee, who had returned from Afghanistan in late April, sat between her older sisters. Today they mourned the death of their mother, who had finally succumbed to the stroke and Alzheimer's.

The stained glass windows diffused light across two red and white carnation sprays, bouquets of pink roses, and scattered greenery displayed at the front of the intimate chapel. A singer began "Wind Beneath My Wings." Three lines into the song, Kacee burst into tears and laid her head against Karon's shoulder. Not only was she grieving the death of her mother, she still grieved the loss of Patrick.

The song also added to the weight of grief still consuming Deborah and Dave. After the service, they eased first from the chapel and walked outside. Dave immediately lit a Marlboro. Deborah gazed beyond the headstones that were sitting on the land across from the parking lot.

"How you doing, babe?" Her husband's voice brought her from the silent moment. He was sitting in one of the high back rockers that were strewn across the long concrete porch with smoke drifting above his head.

"I'm okay, how about you?" Deborah smiled weakly, looking at her husband. Taking a seat in the adjacent chair, she thought how this was much too soon to have to attend another memorial service, to hear some of the same heart-wrenching songs.

"God bless," said the passing woman who had sung "Amazing Grace." Her brown face reflected a sincere smile.

"You, too." Deborah responded with her own smile. The departing guest's soulful rendition of the song had caused chills.

"Aren't you getting too warm out here?" Dave asked his wife with his usual concern.

"I'm okay right now. It's really a beautiful day. I didn't know how pretty Louisiana could be."

Everything was green. Nearby, live oaks reached with enough shade to cover a few dozen people. And the grass lay as green and plush as carpet. Lush elephant ears grew in ditches like a tropical garden. The town of Covington and the narrow roads leading out to places like Felding's held an old southern charm and quietness away from the not too distant interstate.

"Yeah, but it's so hot and humid out here. You'd feel better inside where it's cool."

Dave goaded his wife again as cigarette smoke curled around his face.

Deborah waited a moment before responding. Her husband always showed sincere concern about her comfort and needs, though the one thing she wanted him to do more than anything was to stop smoking. It was a habit he knew he needed to quit. It did not help his heart and circulatory problems, or the 4.2-centimeter aortal aneurysm, a balloon of blood that if ruptured would be equivalent to a grenade exploding inside his body, causing instant death.

A great number of individuals died from rupturing aneurysms they never knew they had. Dave's was discovered by accident after Deborah carried him to the emergency room with severe abdominal pains two weeks after Patrick's memorial. Dave had never been one to complain about pain. But after three days of hurting, he finally said something had to be done. At the hospital the doctor requested a CT scan. Three hours later he returned with the good news that the pain was from an intestinal infection, treatable with antibiotics. The bad news was the discovery of the aneurysm that could not be treated or made to disappear, only monitored. A week later, Deborah and Dave talked with the foremost cardiac surgeon in Columbus about Dave's report.

"There's nothing we can do to shrink it, all we can do is monitor it for growth every six months. If you smoke, you know you shouldn't. You're a grown man; no one should have to tell you that."

The doctor also said that due to the danger, surgery was not an option until an aneurysm reached five centimeters. Statistics showed more individuals lived longer with the culprit than going under the knife.

Deborah left the doctor's office in a daze. She was consumed with anger the moment they walked outside: Dave lit another Marlboro. She withdrew into her shell to keep from exploding, though what she really wanted to do was scream that he *must* want to kill himself. That he must not love her enough to want to quit those godforsaken killers. But that day, she let it go, while smoke swirled over her husband's head and all she could imagine was finding him one day soon, dead from an internal explosion of blood. Some days, all she could see was that the happy world they had been putting back together was falling slowly apart, and Dave didn't seem to care if he lived or died. Deborah's past urging for him to stop had only caused Dave's temper to flare. "It's my only vice for nerves," he always said. The last time the subject arose, they yelled at one another with hateful words. Deborah said he was intentionally trying to shorten his days in the wake of Patrick's death. In his anger, Dave told her that there were days he secretly wished he could.

Deborah finally spoke. "I'll check on Kacee and let her know we'll see her at Kristin's house." She could see through the window that Kacee and her sisters had moved from the chapel into the vestibule. "I'll be back in a few minutes."

Entering the funeral home she spoke to Kacee.

"You okay, sweetie?"

"Yes ma'am. I want you to know how much I appreciate you and Dave being here. I know it's hard on you right now."

"We wouldn't have thought of not being here for you and your sisters. You were all with us. You'll always be a permanent part of our family."

Deborah returned Kacee's smile. She was pretty in the pale blue long sleeved cotton blouse that pulled taut over her small waist and lay flat against her black ankle-length skirt. Her dark, almond shaped eyes, perfectly aligned nose, and full, heart shaped lips that rested on flawless skin were reason enough for Patrick to fall in love with her, even without taking into account the shiny, thick dark hair that lay at her shirt collar. Without doubt, Patrick was looking down from heaven, proud, wishing he could hold his special girl through her newest loss.

"How was your class at school this morning?" Deborah asked.

Kacee was working on her pre-k certification at the college. She had already lined up a teaching position since returning from Afghanistan. She also had plans to obtain her master's degree in early childhood education.

"It was good. I gave my presentation and was outta there."

"Well, I know you need to wrap things up here. Dave and I will see you at Kristin's."

Kacee said, "Okay," as she joined Kristin and Karon to complete the business of their mother's memorial. Deborah knew from her and Dave's recent experience with Patrick's memorial that the girls were about to receive the ashes of the one they had held so close and dear.

Deborah returned to the porch where Dave waited patiently with Marlboro smoke still circling his head.

"You ready to go?" he asked.

"I think I'm more than ready," Deborah said. "Three personal memorial services in four months is about three too many."

After returning to the Comfort Inn to change into jeans and sneakers, Dave and Deborah headed to Kristin's for dinner. Off the main highway Dave turned left onto the two-lane road that meandered by homes of all ages, shapes, and sizes set among a southern tropical alameda.

Twenty miles later he turned left onto Pine Lake Drive. Deborah searched through the thick trees for the first house with blue shutters.

"That's it." She pointed. "I guess the driveway is a bit farther."

Dave turned right next to the mailbox, then right again to pull to the front of the house where several other vehicles were parked, stopping beneath a towering oak. At the front porch, a pleasant great dane dismounted from a bench and greeted them.

"Hey boy, how ya doing?" Dave patted the dog on the head. He thought how Patrick had told him he needed to get a red-tick hound to lounge around with him on the back porch at home.

Deborah knocked on the side of the screen door before entering the house.

"Hey, we made it. You guys live out in the country like we do. It's really beautiful out here." Kristin and Karon were placing food on the table. Kacee was sitting on a stool at the counter separating the kitchen from the family room.

Deborah walked to each woman offering hugs as Dave followed. Then he took a seat in the family room where the television was tuned to the news. America was mourning the death of former President Ronald Reagan. At age ninety-three he, too, had finally succumbed to a long illness and Alzheimer's.

At the counter, Kacee pushed salad around on her plate.

"So, sweetie," Deborah said, facing Kacee from the other side of the counter, "You doing okay?"

"Yeah, I'm actually relieved. Mom didn't need to suffer anymore. How are *you* doing?" Kacee asked.

Deborah looked past Kacee, casting her eyes through the window and into the backyard. She searched for something in the distance that would respond to her next thoughts regarding the loss of Patrick. "Oh, I'm still having good days and bad. It's hard when I think about how we seemed to have everything put back together and have all we ever wanted—two wonderful sons who finally had good futures, and two wonderful women for daughters-in-law—and then we lost him. You lost him."

Deborah tried to restrain the tears. "I dreamed about him last night. Patrick was so vivid. He was home from Iraq. We were all at Epcot in Orlando, just like we planned. I saw him standing in front of all of us, grinning and yelling, 'Come on you guys, let's go! It's fun time.'"

Holding up for the moment, Kacee went to Deborah with a hug. "It's okay," she said and handed Deborah a napkin to wipe her eyes.

"I guess most folks think that because he was my stepson, I'm not as affected by his death."

Kacee hugged Deborah again. "I've always referred to you as Patrick's mom. And you are. He told me that his mother had died when he was seventeen. But when he talked about you, he would say, 'my mom.' I remember after we first met, we talked about books we liked. He said, 'you and my mom will really hit it off. You both like books and you both like kids.'"

"I really appreciate your sharing that." Deborah smiled as mascara left black streaks beneath her eyes. "We all miss him so much. Going to Orlando without him was so hard on Dave. But we wanted to go ahead with plans that were already made. And have fun. Patrick would have wanted that."

"I know he wouldn't want us to sit around crying," Kacee said.

"I know," Deborah said, as she poured a glass of wine. Kacee moved her plate to the other side of the counter.

"I just want you and Dave to know how much he did for me. Even with all that's happened, I'm still thankful we met."

"So, I heard you two met each other at Wal-Mart," Deborah grinned, thinking the question might spark happy memories.

Kacee glanced away from Deborah for a second and then with a sheepish look, told her the truth.

"We actually met online," she said. "Through a match-date service. We didn't want you all to know. We thought you'd think we were nuts or something."

Deborah couldn't help but laugh. "Well, I don't know that I'd ever have the nerve to do something like that, but to each their own. That answers why when we went through Patrick's belongings we found debits from 'Match Up' agency to his old bank account."

"So, you don't think I'm nuts?" Kacee asked.

"Of course not," Deborah said. "Look, we wouldn't be here for each other now if you two hadn't met."

Kacee looked at Deborah with a sigh of relief. "I don't know why I dreaded telling you that. I guess it just sounds so weird or something."

"So, how long was it before you saw one another in person?" Deborah asked.

Kacee thought back to that time in September, well over a year before. "About three weeks," she said. "We only knew what each other looked like from pictures on the web site. We talked over the phone and through instant messaging every night 'till then. We shared our life stories with each other before we ever met."

The memories came flooding back. Patrick had told her he was never married and shared his one love disappointment from the time he lived in California. During the conversations, Kacee could tell he was a confident, self-assured man. He told her he planned on making a career with the Army like his dad had with the Marine Corps.

She told him her life's history and trouble with relationships.

"I figured I'd either scare him off or see what kind of stuff he was really made of," Kacee laughed, looking at Deborah. Then she shared things she had said to Patrick.

Because she needed financial assistance for college, she joined the National Guard when she was twenty. She also married that year, then miscarried by the time she was twenty-one. By twenty-three, her husband said he wanted a divorce; he had met someone else. Kacee had never seen it coming, lost all confidence in herself and faith in believing in love again, until meeting Patrick. She gave him full credit for giving her hope and confidence again, especially after he showed so much patience with her when she became uncertain about staying in the relationship a few months after they finally met in person.

After talking on the phone every day for two weeks, Patrick offered to drive the four hours from Fort Polk to Covington. Kacee didn't want to act anxious, so she put him off another week. Then she told him that if he drove to see her, she wanted him to know beforehand that she had to attend her nephew's Little League baseball game.

"I let him know how important my family was to me," Kacee said. "And nothing kept me from my nephew's baseball or basketball games, if I could help it. And you know, all he said was, 'that's great!' I couldn't believe how easy he was to get along with."

Kacee remembered out loud how Patrick never had a harsh, unreasonable word and why she had been so in love with him. When she recalled the past, her thoughts always went back to *what a man* and the Wednesday night before the 2002 Thanksgiving holiday, when Patrick came by her apartment as she requested, after she had sent him an e-mail saying she didn't want to continue the relationship.

Kacee told Deborah that she was supposed to ride to Georgia with Patrick for the holiday. Instead, she sent him the note and asked him to stop enroute from Fort Polk and pick up the shoes and clothes he had left at her apartment. When she opened her door, he stood holding her key, then asked if she had been crying.

"I asked him if he would come in and talk a few minutes," Kacee said. "Without an angry or hateful attitude, he said 'Sure, no problem,' then he strolled in and sat on the floor cross-legged while I took a seat on the sofa in front of him."

Kacee remembered crying, telling Patrick she didn't know where to start. He simply listened as she spoke.

"I know I've hurt you and I know I need to try and explain myself for sending the note saying I can't see you anymore. All I can tell you is that I get scared when I'm in a relationship. And when certain things begin to happen, like not hearing from you every day, I start thinking about how it'll feel if I get hurt again. So I run. And that's what I'm doing. I'm running before we get in this any further. I just don't think living two hundred miles apart will work."

He listened without saying a word as she told him again everything she could think of about her insecurities, the pain of being hurt from the divorce, bad relationships after that, and even the pain left after the death of her father. She told him she didn't even like herself very much because she knew she did this to herself every time she got close to anyone. Patrick responded with,

"Kacee, you can't be in a relationship unless you like yourself first. You've got to work on getting yourself straight. If you want to get counseling, or talk about anything else, I'm here. Just call me."

Deborah was enthralled by Kacee's story. She was discovering another side of her stepson that she could share with Dave. She wondered if those trips to the counselor in his youth had left Patrick with some positive insight to dealing with situations.

"I couldn't believe my ears," Kacee said. "I've never had anyone, especially a man, speak to me with such caring sincerity. Then he said he'd call me after he returned from Georgia, then I could let him know if I really wanted to split or wanted to keep trying.

"All I could do was sit dumbfounded, thinking, *What kind of man is this? Where did he come from and what have I done?* Then Patrick dismissed himself saying he really had to go because y'all were probably thinking he was halfway there."

Deborah recalled how she had lain awake until the wee hours of the morning before Thanksgiving Day, wondering where Patrick was in the middle of the night. Now she knew why he had arrived home later than planned.

Kacee continued, saying that Patrick had called her, just as he promised. "It was a Friday night and I was out with a friend," she said. "Patrick left four messages on my cell phone and one at my apartment. When I returned his call, the first thing he said was, 'Where were you? I was worried.' After we talked a while, he said, 'I still love you. I'm still willing to try.' And I knew I wanted to do this. I couldn't lose this man."

Deborah watched Kacee's forlorn, red eyes, and felt heartbroken for her. She was glad she could be here to listen and comfort as best she could. Though it brought tears, it brought good memories, too. Deborah was learning just what kind of man her stepson had become, what a good husband and father he would have made. Listening to Kacee's appreciation for Patrick and the comfort she felt with their family left Deborah with no doubt of just how special those 2002 Christmas holidays had been.

"I feel like I've been part of your family forever," Kacee said. "I decided a while back that Patrick had come from good stock."

"Well, I can't take credit for any of his genes," Deborah said. "But, I like to believe I offered *something* that had an impact on his life."

"Well, wherever it came from," Kacee began, "it made him special. One of the most important things Patrick ever said to me concerned my mom. I knew he had to be a keeper when he told me about his real mother's death. And then told me to spend as much time with my mom as possible."

"He did lose his mother too soon," Deborah said. "It was like he never wanted to smile again." She thought of the spirit hawk myth. "I'm so glad he was able to talk to you. It's good when a man can talk. I wish his dad could do that."

Thinking back to those hard years, Deborah couldn't help but feel that Patrick's loss of his mother had spurred the severity of his later problems.

Kacee suggested going down the hall to her bedroom where she and Deborah would be more comfortable and out of hearing distance from the television.

"I'll bring the wine," Deborah said and picked up the Bordolino.

Stepping into the room that Kristin had painted Kacee's favorite color of periwinkle before her return from Afghanistan, Deborah saw the picture of Patrick and Kacee from their 2002 Christmas in Georgia. An eight by ten framed photo of Patrick's unit sat on Kacee's bureau next to a photo of Patrick standing in the Iraqi desert, wearing the sunglasses his dad had mailed him and holding an open Iraqi flag. The same picture sat on the fireplace mantle at home.

There was also a photo of Kacee and Patrick together by the blue waters of the Persian Gulf when they were in Qatar for R&R. Kacee had sent Deborah and Dave a copy of the same one. Sitting on the half-bed against the wall beneath the window, Deborah and Kacee stacked the pillows behind their heads. Deborah asked about the photo of Kacee and Patrick in the forefront of the water. "Is that the day you both left the base to check out the city?"

"That was the day," Kacee said. We went to a mall in Doha. It was awful not to be able to hold hands while we were walking.

But at least we were together. The mall was huge with a skating rink and all kinds of things. We actually stopped at jewelry stores to look at rings. But we couldn't find anything I liked."

"Well, I know he told his dad he was buying you a ring as soon as he returned. He knew he had a good woman."

"I don't know about that," Kacee said, remembering times she had gotten upset with Patrick before he left for Iraq. She wasn't sure she'd ever forgive herself for becoming so upset about things that seemed insignificant now.

Thinking back to Valentine's Day before Patrick left in March, she told Deborah how disappointed and put off she became after other teachers received flowers at work and she didn't. "I figured I'd get a call from Patrick later on that evening," she said. "We had agreed it was too far from Fort Polk to Covington to try to get together for dinner. But then, I didn't even hear from him that night. I was so upset. When he called me the next day to say Happy Valentine's, all I could say was 'Yeah, yeah, yeah,' to let him know I was mad. Then he apologized for having not called me the night before. He said he'd taken duty for another soldier who had a wife and kids. I didn't know whether to believe him or not. I reminded him that we were in a long distance relationship, and I needed to hear from him or my mind started going wild because of my past bad experiences. All he said was, 'you're right. I understand.' And after that, he called or e-mailed me every day just to please me."

"Well, I can tell you this," Deborah said gently. "I remember he called home, knowing you were upset, and told his dad what had happened. All his dad said was, 'Son, I don't know what to tell you.' Dave didn't want to get involved in his son's love life."

"I get so mad at myself for my insecurities, for not always believing in him. I feel so awful at times." Kacee started crying again. Deborah reached to her hand and held it in hers.

"You know, he sent me two Valentine's Day cards this year. They reached me just a few days before he was killed. I don't know if I'd ever be as good as he was. He was so patient. He taught me so much. He taught me how to talk, how to ask for the things I need in a relationship. We communicated every day with e-mails back and forth between Iraq and Afghanistan. When I let him know I was bothered by something, he always responded with the most wonderful messages. He apologized several times for not being able to contact me when he was busy. Now, I feel awful knowing that he was under so much stress, but still listened to me gripe, then sent messages to encourage me while all along I was always safer than he was."

"Honey, Patrick loved you and he knew you loved him. Do you want to stop talking?"

"No," Kacee said, "I need to get things out. I just hate myself for not having enough faith in him."

Deborah moved to the edge of the bed. "Listen, honey, the two of you were under a lot of stress before leaving the country. You have nothing to feel bad about. There's nothing to regret. You've got to believe that."

"I guess you're right," Kacee said. "At least I didn't let him down in Qatar when he was depending on me. He had to leave a day before I did. He told me I better not cry. And I didn't, even though I wanted to bust wide open. Then after he returned to Baghdad, he e-mailed me the most beautiful note, telling me he wanted to be married when we were both back home."

"He loved you, sweetie. And the good memories are the things we'll always have to hold, the gifts he left behind."

"I know," Kacee said, "that's what I keep telling myself. I try to think about the times he called me 'dork' when I did something stupid, so I can laugh. He was just so different from any man I've ever known."

"I have to tell you honey, I always felt that Patrick had potential for being a good communicator, and he always had a good heart." Deborah attempted to turn Kacee's attention away from dwelling on unwarranted guilt, to stories of her own. "He and I spent times talking on and on while his dad just listened. Dave used to say that Patrick and I talked more than he and Patrick. But they finally became best friends. That was a long time coming. There were some difficult times in his life."

Deborah told Kacee about Patrick's years of rebellion, running with the wrong crowds, and her move back to Georgia while Dave remained in California. "I think my leaving California and returning to Georgia may have helped their relationship along. So, I don't believe Dave's and my separation was in vain. It left open space for Dave and Patrick to work on themselves and each other without me in the way. Before then, it was a pretty wild ride at times."

"He told me he'd been a handful in his day," Kacee said.

"At least he told the truth!" Deborah laughed. "I'll never forget some of those times and that first night when he came to live with us, walking into the apartment with a surfboard under one arm and a skateboard under the other. Mad as a hornet that he'd been made to leave Virginia Beach. He was bound and determined to be as mischievous as possible so he'd be sent back to his mother or grandmother. He knew he'd have rules in California instead of running free like he had back there."

Kacee wanted to hear all she could about the man she'd met over a year ago, fallen in love with, and lost. She remembered, again, what Patrick had once said about having some ghosts. She wanted to ask Deborah what he meant, but she didn't have the courage to ask.

"I guess it was tough for him to leave his independent life in Virginia to become part of a controlled environment," Kacee said. "But it sounds like that's what he needed if he was only thirteen. I can't imagine my nephew, Andrew, being that undisciplined."

"It was definitely a new way of living for him. Clean cut hair, curfews, and house chores. We knew he was already smoking, and his dad threatened him if he ever caught him. Of course there were the expectations for better school grades. And oh my lord, having to drag him out of bed every morning to get ready for school after his dad left for work, what a pain. Not to count his skipping school."

Kacee pulled herself to a cross-legged sitting position on the bed.

"Well, I know Patrick always talked about how he wanted to make his dad proud," Kacee said, rubbing her index finger around the mouth of the empty wine glass.

"I know. That's what Captain Corn and First Sergeant Maggard told us after Patrick died. Everything they told us about Patrick is what Dave and I will carry the rest of our days. Where Patrick and others like him are concerned, there's never been a more appropriate saying than, 'It isn't how a person begins their life, it's how they end it.' And I'm so glad he reached that point. It's the greatest gift he could have left his dad. I think it shows how he matured and realized the pain he had caused Dave over the years. I think he wanted to make up for as much as he could."

Kacee still wanted to know what Patrick had meant about ghosts. She waited to see if Deborah would eventually let it out.

Dave looked around for Deborah and Kacee.

"Anybody seen those two talkers?" he asked the remaining group in the family room.

"I think they went to Kacee's room," Kristin said.

Dave walked down the hall to make sure they were both okay. He'd seen a few tears from both of them.

"Yeah, babe, we're okay, thanks. Go back to your guy thing," Deborah said, with a kiss to his cheek.

Before leaving, Dave asked Kacee to show him where Patrick's television and other belongings were. By May, after Kacee's return from Afghanistan, Patrick's unit had also returned to Fort Polk. By invitation, she attended Eagle Troop's family picnic. Deborah and Dave missed going since Dave had shoulder surgery the week before. Patrick's best buddy, Bob, had kept Patrick's television and several other boxes. Bob had loaded them into Kacee's car before she left the base following the gathering.

"The TV is in the family room behind a chair. And the boxes are in the back of my car."

"I can carry the TV," Deborah said, as they walked together to the front of the house. "Dave's shoulder won't allow him to lift much yet."

"I'll get that for you." Kacee's older nephew lifted the nineteen-inch television and followed Dave to the Pathfinder. Deborah and Kacee walked to Kacee's car where she popped open the trunk lid. They each lifted a box of unknown contents and carried them to Dave.

"By the way," Deborah asked Kacee, "did you find out from Bob where the nickname Cookie came from for Patrick?"

Kacee laughed. "Sure did. It stuck after the two of them went fishing. Patrick set a camp stove up on a sandbar to cook some fish they caught. Bob said he told Patrick not to do something or other regarding the way he was starting the fire. Then Patrick told him he knew what he was doing, he'd been a restaurant cook for years before the Army. All of a sudden the flames jumped sky high from the camp stove causing Patrick to jump and fall in the water. Bob said he told Patrick, "Okay, Cookie, so you know what you're doing, huh?"

"They were good friends, weren't they? I think Patrick called him Mountain Bob because he was from the hills of Kentucky," Dave added.

"I think that's what I heard," Deborah said, handing Dave another box to put in the back of the SUV.

Deborah walked next to Kacee as she closed her car trunk. "Do you feel like walking? I need to work off some of that wine I gorged myself on."

"Sure," Kacee said.

The late afternoon felt cooler. Kacee's eleven-year-old nephew, Andrew, was running from the house to his dad's car. He wore his baseball uniform and carried his glove. He had gone to all the adults and invited them to come and watch his all-star catching and pitching.

"Look's like Andrew and his dad are off to the ball field," Deborah said, watching the two of them get inside the Camaro. "I bet they're close, aren't they?"

Kacee looked at the ground as she and Deborah walked to the backyard. "Yep, Clay is very close and very protective of Andrew. Especially since Brian died."

"I remember Kristin telling me in February that she and Clay had lost a son."

Walking close to Kacee, Deborah thought about, could feel, the turmoil that Kristin and Clay had gone through when their three-year-old son died. She even wondered if the pain were in any way different when losing a young child as opposed to losing a grown one. It didn't really matter, Deborah thought. It was an indescribable pain that left an indescribable vacuum. Only a parent who had lost a child could truly comprehend what another parent felt.

"How did Brian die?" Deborah asked.

In the backyard, Kacee stopped a distance from the swimming pool that was close to the house. Her dad had built the pool when she was seven.

"He drowned in that pool, eight years ago. None of us except Andrew and his friends swim in it anymore."

"Oh my God," Deborah said, staring at the clear water.

"Brian had been taking swimming lessons that summer. He loved the water."

Deborah and Kacee sat down in the swing on the far end of the thirty-foot pool.

"My niece, Carla, found him floating in the water. She was only eleven. The report said that Brian hit his head. We all believe that while everyone was cleaning up the front yard, he went inside the house, changed into his swimsuit and got his floaties. He was always so independent. He was changing his own clothes by the time he was two. Anyway, the floaties were in the water, but not on him. He must have been running, fell and hit his head on the concrete, then landed in the water.

"Oh, Kacee, I am so sorry. Your family has been through so much. I don't know what to say."

"Everybody blamed themselves for one reason or the other. I even blamed myself, knowing that if I'd been at the house that morning I would've kept him glued to me," Kacee said, crossing her ankles one over the other, then reaching down to pick a blade of grass.

A slight breeze moved the air around the two women. A squirrel scampered up the pine tree that sat at the end of the house, and a neighbor's horse whinnied in the adjoining pasture.

"If I had been there, I know it wouldn't have happened. But I wasn't."

"That word *if* is the biggest two letter word in the dictionary," Deborah said, pushing her heels into the ground enough to give the swing a gentle sway.

"If we sat around thinking of every horrific situation that wouldn't have been *if* we'd done one tiny single thing differently, we'd all be crazier than what we already think we are." Deborah looked towards the calm, blue sky. "And needless to say, none of it is in our hands. *If* the crew of the Titanic had seen the iceberg sooner, all those folks wouldn't have died. *If* Dave had not changed guard duty with another soldier in Vietnam, it would have been him who died that night from incoming fire. *If* Patrick had given up firing at the insurgents while on patrol that night in Baghdad, more men would have died with him. *If* Patrick hadn't joined the Army he may still be alive, but still running with the wrong crowd with no direction for his life. If, if, if... I guess I don't believe in going through *if* scenarios after the fact of a bad situation. But I do enjoy knowing the good things that happen that wouldn't have *if* an event hadn't caused it. *If* Patrick hadn't met you we wouldn't have one another right now. And I feel like Dave and I have gained a daughter."

"And because of Patrick, I feel like I have another set of parents," Kacee smiled again.

"It's just the way the universe runs," Deborah said, keeping the sway with the swing. "Deep down, I don't believe there are any mistakes even though I ask 'why' at times, knowing it's all rhetorical, and I still get angry."

"I know everything happens for a purpose," Kacee said. She shifted in the swing and played with the silver ring on her right hand. "I know things and timing doesn't always make sense. But I've learned to hold onto my faith, which is something I didn't do for a long time after my dad died."

"That's understandable," Deborah said, patting Kacee on the knee. "And you were so young to have to deal with that. I'm waiting for the day we can all make sense of everything."

Deborah folded her arms across her chest and pushed her heel against the ground to make the swing sway again. Lightening bugs flashed off and on around the yard as dusk approached.

"I've told God I'm angry, but I'm still asking for help to get through all this. Sitting and dwelling with anger without asking for help to overcome it only creates a heavy, heavy burden, an abyss. I've tried to explain this to Dave, but he still doesn't want to hear it. I guess what I really get down about is that God didn't let us enjoy more of Patrick's life after he had begun accomplishing more, had more self-esteem than ever, and was such a joy. His commanding officers have told us that he had more friends and was one of the best leaders they'd ever seen in their military careers. If they only knew how ironic his life was, the miracle that he was. But on the other hand, I sometimes think about what this war might have done to him. How he might have turned in the opposite direction again once he was back home. No one knows what a war can do to a man or a woman."

"I know," Kacee sighed, and pushed her hair behind her ears. "All we can do without going nuts is hold onto faith. After Mom died all I could say was, 'God, I can't take anymore. First it was Dad, then Brian, then Patrick, and now Mom. If you're there, please lift this burden I'm feeling.' And you know, the burden left. I still get sad, but I don't feel the heaviness in my shoulders, or a darkness."

"I know. I just wish I could get Dave to understand this. It's really hard when only one of a couple wants to talk about faith. It leaves an uncomfortable space in the relationship. I feel I'm carrying the both of us. And I know I'm guilty of not letting go and letting God work things out. I get frustrated so easily. I know I've questioned, 'Why pray?' just as Dave has. But I think I've really come to understand the Lord's Prayer. It's not about praying for our will to be done. It's all about God's will, even though we don't understand it when we're in pain from grief or sickness. Or we keep seeing war and famine. I've come to realize that the praying is to gain the power to get through the bad times, to find good in the aftermath."

"I believe that," said Kacee. "I can smile a bit again since Patrick's death. Although I feel guilty when I do."

"I know. Sometimes I think Dave thinks I don't care or grieve when I try to laugh or dwell on something other than Fox News. Then on one of my down days, I heard a speaker on a public service channel who perked me up a bit. He had this great line that just fell into me and lifted my spirit. He said, 'We are not human beings having a spiritual experience. We are spiritual beings having a human experience.' Then he went on to talk about how the reason we fall into feelings of darkness and depression at times. We forget to stop and remember that we emanated from the perfect power of the universe, and if we reunite with that spirit through prayer or meditation, then the darkness in our spirit will lift."

The sun had drifted from sight and the only light came from the windows of the house, a corner spotlight, and a full moon. Deborah looked for the North Star and the Big Dipper.

"I like that," Kacee said, smiling. "When you think about things from that perspective, it makes sense. I think I'll put that on my refrigerator door when I move into my apartment. 'I am not a human being having a spiritual experience, I am a spiritual being having a human experience.' Yeah, I like that."

By eleven that night, Deborah and Kacee had shared one story after the other and cried enough to fill a good size pail while Dave and members of Kacee's family had remained engrossed with television and the Lakers and Pistons game.

"Well, who won?" Deborah asked, walking back with Kacee into the family room.

"The Lakers won in overtime, ninety-eight to ninety-one, but there's three more games left. The Pistons still have time to get their act together and win the championship," Dave said.

Kacee stood hands on her hips, with the smile she always managed to find. "I can't believe you don't like the Lakers after all the years you lived in California."

"They were Patrick's team. I always chose the team they played, even if I didn't like them."

"So, you ready to go, now?" Deborah nudged Dave, turning him in the direction of the door so they could return to the hotel.

After saying goodnight, they drove along the unfamiliar two-lane road toward the Comfort Inn. Deborah saw a shooting star fall across the sky. She squeezed her husband's hand. In all their years, small talk as they rode together, even for hours, was not something that happened often. It was as though they went deep inside themselves while the odometer counted the miles, but they had a habit of laying a hand across the other's thigh or entwining their fingers together in the center of the seat, all they needed when words weren't available. What Deborah hoped for these days was that her affection would calm the anger in Dave that no words could touch.

Dave's thoughts were on Kacee's nephew, Andrew. He had enjoyed picking on the eleven-year-old about the basketball game. Andrew had wanted the Lakers to win, just as Patrick always did. Dave drifted to Patrick's young face, always grinning, restless, and eager to showoff. He thought of days of the Boy's Club, karate, and Little League football, running on Virginia Beach with their white German shepherd, fishing together off Chesapeake Bay or digging for clams. Watching him surf or performing handstands on a skateboard. And finally seeing him a content man in uniform after many misdirected years. Dave didn't believe the incredible pain, the immense vacuum, would ever disappear.

Hearing Dave sigh, Deborah looked at him in the glow of the dash lights.

"You okay?"

"Yeah, just a little tired. How about you?"

"Same here," Deborah said, reaching to open the moon roof.

What a view, she thought, staring upward into the night sky, a well of deep blue ink with diamonds scattered across the top. She reached her hand through the open roof and let the warm night air race against it as the vehicle moved sixty miles an hour through the darkness.

~ SIXTEEN ~

AFTER DRIVING SIX HOURS from Covington, Dave stopped at the mailbox and retrieved three days' worth of mail and newspapers. A glance at the envelopes showed condolence cards from acquaintances in Southern California.

"What'd we get?" Deborah asked, taking the bundle of mail from her husband so he could drive down the hill to the garage.

"Just a bunch of junk mail and more cards. I think I saw something from Kacee, too."

"There's still a lot of good folks in the world," Deborah said, flipping through the envelopes.

As Dave turned off the engine, Deborah looked at him and smiled. "Looks like this one from Kacee is something special. It's addressed only to you. You want to open it?"

"I'll open it after we unload the car," Dave said as he walked to the back of the vehicle to remove the luggage.

Deborah walked a couple of steps to where Dave stood and planted a quick kiss on his cheek.

"Hey, can I have another one?" he said, as Deborah scooted around him to go in the house.

"Maybe, after while. I'm going in to check the phone messages."

While Deborah headed to the answering machine in her home office, Dave carried the two bags to the bedroom. Returning to the family room, he picked up Kacee's envelope from the coffee table and went to the back porch. With a cigarette between his lips and the envelope opened, he pulled out the green and gold card that said *For a Father Who Means So Much*. He unfolded a letter that read:

Dear Dave,

I hope you do not mind the way I chose to express myself...

I just want you to know that this is the first time since I was eleven years old that I have had the opportunity or/and desire to celebrate Father's Day. THANK YOU! (When I was married, I did not even wish my father-in-law happy father's day, if that tells you anything!)

About a month ago, when I was trying to find the perfect card to express how much you mean to me, I kept Patrick in mind. I know he would have chosen a card for you that expressed his love and gratitude for you in the same way. How do I know this? I know this because of the way Patrick expressed his feeling for you through the Instant Message conversations while we were overseas. Not only that, his eyes would beam when he spoke of his job in the military and I know his calling was to follow your footsteps by proudly serving our country. He was proud to be the son of a retired Marine Corps sergeant major.

Thank you and Deborah again for being there when I needed you most.

Love,

Kacee

Dave blinked back the tears filling his eyes. After putting the card back in the envelope and placing it on the deck railing, he lit another Marlboro. A couple of squirrels scampered across the grass next to the porch. He hated the way they dug holes in his yard, burying hickory nuts and other goods. Deborah had attempted to teach him to look at nature differently. She had told him that squirrels symbolized planning in advance for tough times, gathering what was needed for sustaining life, ignoring the rest. She said the resourceful animals set an example for sorting through belongings and beliefs.

Maybe there was something to it, he thought, *maybe not.* He was trying to sort through the past months; he had lots of sorting to go through with God. His family had reconciled at this home, bringing his greatest happiness. Now it was the home of his worst nightmare. But it was where he'd live the rest of his life. He had told Deborah, "This is where I'll die and you're gonna bury me."

He had traveled around the world during his twenty-eight years with the Marines; he couldn't care less if he ever went anywhere else. He had truly fallen in love with this place. The back and side yards looked like a rain forest when the trees and shrubs sagged with foliage and formed a canopy. Deborah had added azaleas in the bare areas beneath the trees, and baskets of impatiens that hung from limbs. After Patrick's memorial she had charged with all her might into the brick-hard clay with a shovel and post hole digger, adding more plants. She had dug more holes with added screaming after finding out about his aneurysm.

But mostly, Dave loved watching his wife perched on the deck in the mornings, rocking in silence, drinking her coffee, reading, writing, or watching the green anole lizards run back and forth on the deck railing. She was everything to him, and without her he truly wouldn't have one damn reason to want to go on. Even though he told her every day, "I love you," he wasn't sure she realized the depth of that love. She had made this a home to be enjoyed and loved for the rest of their lives, and was helping him the best she could to pick up the shattered pieces. He just didn't know how to say to her what sat in his heart.

Dave turned to watch two more squirrels challenge each other for the seeds in the feeder on the oak tree. The dominant one chased the lesser toward the top of the limbs. He took another drag from his Marlboro and gazed toward the lower deck, where the Jacuzzi emitted a low murmur. He remembered one of the last conversations he had with Patrick, no more than a week before he died.

"I can't get clean, Dad. I'm filthy all the time. It's so dirty here."

"Well, in another month, when you get home, you'll get clean. Deborah bought a Jacuzzi so you and Jason can sit and enjoy Coronas with Kacee and Sindy."

"That's gonna be nice," Patrick said. "I'm ready to come home."

"Well, son, it won't be long, about thirty more days. Just keep yourself covered. Keep your head down. Don't ever let your guard down. Not until you're on U.S. soil."

Dave had repeated those words more than once to his son. He knew a soldier was never out of danger until the plane landed in the states.

The day Dave left Vietnam his unit was under enemy fire at Dong Ha during the Tet Offensive. U.S. planes never came to a complete stop on the airstrip. On the day he left, he had run faster than ever and dropped his duffle bag to reach the back of a moving C-123. Sometimes he wondered at the miracle of making it back home. That plane could have been brought down before it ever left Vietnam airspace.

Dave's final words at the end of the last call with Patrick were as usual, "Keep your head down, Son. I love you." And Patrick never failed to return, "I love you, Dad. And tell Deborah I love her, too."

Dave felt the tears well in his eyes. *Why, God, why? Why did you take my boy just when he had found a good life he loved?* He squeezed his eyes together, tight, to push back the tears, his lips quivered around his cigarette.

He remembered when they lived in Southern California, when Patrick was twenty-one. It was one of those times after Patrick asked to live at home again. A neighbor came to the house and told him that Patrick was sitting in an alley five miles away, threatening to kill himself. The neighbor worked at a camera shop at Seaside Strip Mall in Oceanside, a known drug area. Leaving the shop that day, the man saw Patrick and talked to him. All Patrick could do was cry and repeat over and over that he was going to kill himself. After receiving the information, Dave drove to the strip mall, found Patrick, and took him to the hospital. This was the first time Dave had actually confirmed that Patrick had crossed the line with drugs. His worst fears were confirmed at the hospital that day. Patrick was a heroin user.

He and Deborah had been suspicious that Patrick used marijuana. After coming to live with them when he was thirteen, he had all the signs. But they could never find the proof. They had battled his rebellious behavior, skipping school, and poor grades. Dave made excuses because Patrick had been an ADD child taking Ritalin. Or he was too rough on him when he caught him in a lie, like the day one of the neighbors said Patrick stole beer from their patio.

After taking him to the hospital, the next step was drug rehab at an old farm in the hills, sixty miles from San Diego.

When Deborah and Dave were allowed to visit, Patrick showed them the vegetable gardens that the men who lived there grew for food. They met other young men struggling to overcome their deadly habits. They saw the room where they met to talk about their problems with one another, the kitchen where Patrick cooked. Then Dave remembered the day when Patrick called, saying he had been kicked out because one of the other guys picked a fight with him, so they were both removed from the program. Patrick had always been passive. Not one to pick a fight or really fight back. Dave had felt angry about the dismissal, but drove to the mountains to get his son.

Patrick returned home making promises that he was clean and life would be different. But for seven more years he was in and out of the house, and back and forth to North Carolina, Virginia Beach, Miami, or someplace else. Dave and Deborah argued about his coming and going and not improving his life. Somewhere during that time Patrick met Rena and they moved together into an apartment. Two years later, with a broken heart, Patrick took off to Tahoe, where he cooked at a resort kitchen and spent the rest of his time snowboarding. Dave and Deborah visited there once. Deborah stood shocked when she saw Patrick's hair knotted in dread locks and wearing as many ear hoops as he could fit on his lobes. A tattoo encircled each arm above the elbow. After that, Patrick rarely came home, even for Christmas.

Deborah had finally tired of the ups and downs and their arguments that finally led to living in more silence than anything. Dave never realized how he had lost interest in anything fun or energetic. He was content to exist in front of the television when not at work. Deborah finally decided that for her own self-preservation she had to return to Georgia. After sixteen years she needed to live near her own son.

During the first year she was gone, Patrick returned from Tahoe. He lived with friends and then with Dave. Dave bought his son a used Nissan so Patrick would have a way back and forth to his job at Wolfgang Puck's restaurant. After ten months, for reasons only he knew, he left Puck's to work for Crabby Joe's restaurant at the beach. Patrick had sworn there were no more drugs in his life, something Dave always believed or pretended to believe when Patrick said it. But a number of months after starting work for Crabby Joe's everything went south again. After working as a counselor for Orange County Juvenile Probation, Dave was well aware of the signs of black tar heroin. And when he finally noticed that Patrick's hands carried the black stains gained from rolling cigarettes with the deadly drug, he confronted him. Every angry emotion exploded that night.

"Get out, and don't come back, ever!" he had shouted at Patrick. "I've had all I can deal with. Get off those fucking drugs and stay off, or don't ever show your face to me again!"

For years, Dave denied his son's addictions. He always wanted to believe that the stereo systems, music CDs, and diamond ring that had disappeared from the house were stolen by some of Patrick's visiting acquaintances. Now his wife was gone and Patrick had let him down once more.

A month later, Patrick called. "The car is broken down," he said. "What do you want me to do with it?"

"Where are you?" Dave asked.

"I'm at the strip mall on the boulevard," Patrick said, with his usual, passive tone. No one had ever heard as much as a loud yell or angry scream from him.

"I'll be there in a few minutes. Stay where you are."

Dave drove to the mall and parked next to his son who was leaning against the black Pulsar, puffing on a cigarette. With shaggy hair and wearing wrinkled shorts and a t-shirt, it was obvious he had lived in his car for a month.

Dave shut off his engine and stepped from his pickup.

"Hey, Son."

"Hey, Dad."

As the two embraced, Dave patted his son. Patrick was too thin. "Listen, Son, I love you."

"I love you, too."

"Why Son? Why do you do this to yourself? Why do you have to get messed up with these drugs?"

"I'm a weak person, Dad. That's all I can say. I'm just weak, and when I get around somebody that's got 'em, I can't seem to say no."

Dave held his son by the shoulders and looked him in the eyes. "I'm going to have the car towed to a repair shop to find out what's wrong. Then you can come home with me. But I swear Patrick, one more sign of drugs and you're out for good. Do you understand me? No more after this if you screw up. No more."

Patrick gazed back with, "Yeah, I understand."

Dave had never been sure as to what brought about Patrick's next steps. Was it prayer? Was it tough love? Was it fate? Did Patrick finally just get tired of hitting concrete walls? Who knows the answers to why people change, for the bad or good? Dave was just thankful that Patrick's life took a turn for the better.

After coming back home, Patrick found another job at a restaurant not far from the house. Dave thought he was kidding when four months later he talked about joining the Army. He would mention he was thinking about enlisting, then he wouldn't say anything for days. Then he would bring it up again. Finally, needing approval, he straight out asked one day, "Dad, do you care if I join the Army?"

Dave was a Marine. He figured that's why Patrick wanted his blessing. All he could say was, "Son, I don't care which one you join, just please get a direction for your life. The military is a good one. It was good for me. It saved my life."

Within a couple of days, Dave escorted a clean-shaven Patrick to the recruiter's office.

"I don't have my high school diploma," he told the sergeant who was ready to add him to his quota.

"No problem there, I can get you to the adult education program for your GED."

Dave believed that Patrick's love for reading history, science, geography, and military information, along with his loads of real-world experience had somewhat prepared him for the testing. His son had lived the first thirteen years of his life around Washington, D.C., the Norfolk naval base in Portsmouth, Virginia, where he was born, and Oceana Naval Air Station, where the Navy's most sophisticated aircraft landed and took off. From age thirteen Patrick had been around the military life at Camp Pendleton. And Miramar was not far from Oceanside, where Deborah and he had taken Patrick for the annual air shows. Patrick had always had a strong interest in planes and jets and would watch anything about them that aired on television. Deborah had always said that Patrick had a load of potential, if he would just use it.

The recruiter had been shocked to discover that Patrick was twenty-nine.

"Yeah, I'm a late bloomer," he said with a laugh. "I guess it's better late than never."

"You've got that right," the recruiter grinned.

Dave remembered that Patrick had kept the promise he made. He had dropped, cold turkey, any drugs he had been using. After a passing conversation with a local cop, he assisted with undercover work to bust a few drug dealers around his old stomping grounds. With help from his recruiter, a clear mind, and a goal that he had set sight to, he brushed up on algebra and English. A few weeks later he tested with high scores on his G.E.D. and took his oath to the Army.

It was during those last months that Dave could see the similar parallels between his son and himself. After all, his drug of choice had been alcohol from the time he was a teenager until he was twenty-two and finally decided that liquor, dead-end jobs, and being a high school drop-out were taking him exactly nowhere. With the draft looking him in the face, he had decided to join the Marine Corps because they had the best looking uniform and were the toughest. He'd been the local "cool but tough guy" in his day. The quiet, bad boy who wouldn't start a fight, but could end one thumbs up if he needed to. His recruiter had been sent to pick him up for boot camp while he was in Panama City, Florida, enjoying a party. He was drunk when he stepped on the bus to Parris Island. He'd gotten his GED in a bunker in Vietnam.

Two weeks after Patrick's swearing in, Dave saw his son off from the San Diego airport. He was headed for boot camp at Fort Knox, Kentucky. Patrick had been at basic training for seven weeks when Dave received a distressing call.

"Dad, I've injured my knee in a training exercise. I'm on crutches. I've been recycled to start all over again with another platoon. I'm afraid I'm not gonna make it."

Dave could hear the appeal in his son's voice to contact the captain and talk about the situation.

"Son, I don't know what I can do."

"Dad, I've come so far. I'm five weeks away from graduating. If I have to start all over again... I just don't know."

"Son, I'll do what I can. I'll call the captain and talk to him. But don't get your hopes up. Just hang in there. If you have to start over, I know you can make it."

Dave wrote down the phone number Patrick gave for the commanding officer. The next morning he contacted Captain Austin. After introducing himself as the father of the recruit, Patrick Tainsh, and also a retired Marine Corps sergeant major, he pleaded his case. He told the CO that he knew Patrick had hurt his knee and was being recycled to start over.

"Captain," Dave said, "I know that you have your rules and reasons for doing what you do. I was a part of the system for twenty-eight years. But this is so important to my son. He's never been motivated for anything in his life like he is for this. Please consider letting him complete his training with his old platoon."

Dave listened to the captain explain that they were concerned that Patrick would re-injure himself if they allowed him to continue on course and that next time it could be worse.

Dave told him, "Sir, for his sake, please let's take that chance this time. He'll be crushed if he has to start all over again."

"I'll give the situation further thought and see how your son's injury is coming. I'll let you know, Sergeant Major."

"Thank you, sir; I appreciate your looking into this."

In two days, Dave received the news that Patrick had been allowed to return to his original platoon to continue training. At the end of twelve weeks, Dave drove to Fort Knox and attended Patrick's graduation, learning he would go for duty at Fort Polk, Louisiana. No father and son in the world were ever happier or prouder to have moved beyond the road that had been long and hard for them. Finally, Patrick had turned the corner, climbing from the grip of a dark cave.

This is what angered Dave now. After Patrick finally found the sunlight that had drawn him into a fulfilling new life, Dave felt that God had still let both Patrick and him down. God had not answered his prayers to return Patrick home safely from Iraq. And as much as *that* anger ate at Dave, anger at himself was no less for the times he had been so rough on his son and the times he had kicked him from the house.

"You okay, honey?" Deborah called from the door before walking next to her husband. When he turned his face toward her, she could tell he had been far away into disturbing thoughts.

"Yeah, I'm okay. Kacee sent a really nice card. You can read it if you want to." Dave handed his wife the envelope. "Did we have any phone messages?"

"There was one from Patrick's first sergeant. He and his wife are on leave and traveling. He wanted to know if they could drop by and visit us this Saturday. I left a message on their cell phone telling them that'd be great."

"Sounds good. Let's go inside, the mosquitoes are eatin' me up," Dave said, crushing another spent cigarette.

~ SEVENTEEN ~

AT THREE P.M. ON SATURDAY, June 12, 2004, Deborah answered the phone call from First Sergeant Robert Maggard and gave directions to reach her home. He and his family had driven from Fort Polk through Florida then to Georgia, making their way to South Carolina to visit relatives before heading to a new duty station in Texas. Deborah was standing outside with Dave when the silver SUV came down the driveway. Patrick had always spoken highly of his senior sergeant. Deborah and Dave had met Rob's wife, Barb, at Patrick's memorial service at Fort Polk, Louisiana, in February.

Rob, about forty, looked exactly the way a career soldier should: clean cut and in shape. The past year in Iraq had not left him looking too worn on the outside.

While Dave and Rob spoke to one another, Deborah met Barb with a hug. Seeing the two teenagers sitting in the backseat, she invited them to get out.

"Let's go inside where it's a little cooler," Dave said. "I think the chairs will be more comfortable than standing around."

Inside the family room, Dave showed Rob the oak and glass cabinet he had custom-made to hold Patrick's military awards, photos, saber, spurs, and Stetson. Deborah and Barb took seats across the room from one another. Barb and Rob's fifteen-year-old daughter stood next to her mother. Their seventeen-year-old son sat in a corner of the sofa.

"So, I bet it's great to have your dad home," Deborah said, directing her attention to the youths. But what she wanted most was to talk to Rob about Patrick. She and Dave needed to hear about Patrick's last months from someone who had been with him. After Dave took a seat on the sofa, Deborah moved the conversation to Rob who was seated in the rocker across the room.

"We just want you to know how much we appreciate your coming to see us. It really means a lot to be able to talk to someone who spent time with Patrick this past year," Deborah said.

The soldier, looking like any everyday civilian in blue jeans and a t-shirt, leaned forward with his fingers entwined with one another. He told Deborah and Dave that he felt he had to see them and share anything he could about Patrick's life in the months before his death. One thought soon led to another, from the humor that Patrick had brought to the unit to his die-hard dedication.

"If he could, he would talk forever about surfing," Rob said, with a slight grin on his face. "He was so laid back with that California surfer attitude. But he was one of the best, most dedicated scouts the Army could have asked for. Every time we returned from a patrol, he'd hound me about what he could do better. He'd go over everything that'd been done and look for better ways to handle the next mission. There were times I'd have to tell him, 'Tainsh, you already do it the best, there's nothing else I can tell you! Get some rest!'"

Deborah watched her husband smile with pride. They both managed to laugh as Rob Maggard told stories. They also shared a few stories of their own about Patrick's rebellious adolescent years and his dislike of school. But they left out the part about the Army saving Patrick from an almost fatal drug habit.

"He told me he'd been a handful when he was a kid," Rob said. This brought up a few pointers to Rob's son, that his dad and mom weren't the only parents who hounded their kids about education and responsibility. Finally, Deborah found the courage to ask the question that Dave and she needed an answer to. She had rolled over and over in her head how to pose it to Rob. She knew from experience with Dave that battle-worn soldiers didn't like being asked about their wartime experiences. But Dave and she both needed to know exactly what had happened the night Patrick was killed. One death certificate had said throat wound, another said gunshot. With as much nerve as she could muster, searching for the appropriate way, Deborah finally said to Rob, "I know I probably shouldn't ask you this. I know certain things are not good to talk about, but if you'll forgive me, we'd like to know if you could tell us what happened that night."

Dave's face grew somber. He supported the question to his son's first sergeant. Rob looked at both of them with gentle somberness in his rugged, tanned face.

"Sergeant Major," he said, "first I want you to know that Patrick's greatest wish was to make you proud. He was always saying, 'I've got to make my dad proud.' When he was asked one time about going to school to become a warrant officer, he said, 'No thanks, my dad retired a sergeant major, and that's what I'm gonna do.' You were the most important person to him. And believe me, he was an outstanding soldier. He was like a magnet. Other troops came to him for advice and friendship. He was the superior example of a soldier and leader. His reputation always preceded him. He was a commanding officer's dream."

Dave and Deborah sat quietly, holding back tears, ready to hear the painful words that would become Patrick's legacy.

"I can tell you exactly what happened that night. I was there with him."

Feeling nausea at what she was about to hear, Deborah also saw the moisture forming in Rob's eyes and the color draining from her husband's face.

"We were based at Baghdad International. On 11 February, about 2200 hours, we headed out on patrol with a four-vehicle convoy. Your son was on the third vehicle. He was the gunner on the CO's Humvee. We hadn't gone more than a couple of miles from the airport on a road running parallel to a canal. Sergeant Tainsh was always observant from his position. He let the CO know he had spotted some guys hanging out, talking on the other side of the canal. The convoy halted to observe the situation. In order to change position for observing behind us, the convoy needed to turn and go back. When the first vehicle moved to swing into the turn, a roadside bomb exploded, throwing the first vehicle into a wall, killing the driver instantly, and injuring another soldier.

This was a trick the radicals had learned to use to hit us. They would draw attention to themselves to get a convoy to halt and then detonate the explosive device."

Deborah watched Rob turn his eyes to the floor as he continued speaking. She could only imagine what it was taking for the man to speak memories she had no doubt he would rather keep sealed, locked away from memory.

"When the bomb went off, Sergeant Tainsh began immediately to lay down fire against the insurgents. By then they were lying on the ground on the other side of the canal, sending RPG fire against the convoy. The back of my vehicle took a hit while I was running to the number one vehicle with the medic. I could hear Sergeant Tainsh firing round after round from his fifty-caliber. At least ten other soldiers were taking fire while your son must have fired over four hundred rounds so they could get to safety. Then I heard the CO on the radio yelling for me to get to his vehicle. He kept saying, 'Help Tainsh, help Tainsh.' I thought he needed my assistance with coordinates or something. By the time I reached the CO, Sergeant Tainsh was lying with his head in the captain's lap. What the captain had wanted was for me to bring the medic to help your son. After he had lain down enough fire to rid the area of the insurgents and have everyone safe, Sergeant Tainsh slipped inside the vehicle and tapped Captain Corn on the shoulder, telling him 'Sir, I've been hit.' Then he slumped onto the captain, who was still holding him when I got there. We could see him bleeding from the neck area. We lay him on the ground beside the vehicle and the medic saw to him immediately. But he was already gone. After we got him to the hospital, the doctors said that he had been hit in the throat by a piece of shrapnel that penetrated through his neck and came out through his back. They said he should have been down instantly. He should have never been able to fire all those rounds with a wound like that. But because he did, I'm alive with those other men, sir. He's a true hero."

By the end of the reliving, tears ran down everyone's face. Deborah noticed how the lines in her husband's face seemed more prevalent than ever. It had been as hard to listen to the words as it was for Rob to say them.

"You'll never know what this meant to us," Dave said. "I know this was hard for you."

"Sir, it's the least I could do for you. Sergeant Tainsh will never be forgotten. That's why the CO recommended him for the Silver Star."

Dave stood from his seat on the sofa and clasped Robert Maggard's hands. No further words were required. Moments later he and Deborah watched the SUV disappear from sight, while the last ten minutes of Patrick's life remained an imprint branded against their souls.

~ EIGHTEEN ~

THE NIGHT AFTER THE Maggards' visit, Deborah slept on the sofa again. In the pre-dawn morning, tears streaming down her face, she pulled herself from a frightening dream. A Humvee was upside down in mid-air in the dark of night. Shaking, Deborah wiped the tears from her face, praying to God to lift the weight from her soul. He was the only one she had to talk to about any of this except for Kacee. But Kacee was in another state. Deborah never approached Dave to talk about her dreams or feelings for fear it would upset him. She lived with anger because she couldn't get him to talk with her; she faced the same problem they'd had all the years they'd been married, a reason she had left him those years ago. He still never said anything to her about his deepest thoughts. He had slowly opened some of the boxes that held Patrick's life, hung his clothes on hangers, and placed them in the closet in the guest bedroom. She had seen him brush back tears. What she wanted to see him do was hold to her, let it out, scream if he wanted to.

But all his life he had been trained to remain in control. Keep it inside. Don't let anyone see your weakness. Deborah had told him over and over again, "It's okay, honey. Cry, scream, do something. But get it out." But what usually came was a battle of words that would begin over nothing and mean nothing, like the day he exploded because she'd been in town longer than she expected and didn't call home. Or his telling her she didn't have to live there with him if she couldn't take the way he spent his hours staring at the television and chain smoking. In return, she'd shouted and cried.

"I'll never leave my home again," she had said. If you can't confide in me, then maybe you need to drive to California or someplace until you work through all this. If you decide I'm worth living for or find you need me for something other than a caretaker, then I'll be here when you return. But living together, snarling and clawing at one another at the drop of a pin is not going to help either of us."

What made things worse were the mornings when she woke up feeling as though she were tied inside a dark bag weighted down by concrete. Her nerves would lie on the top of her skin like sparking electrical wires, waiting for something to touch, ignite, and explode to remove the feeling. For years, these outbreaks of nerves had overwhelmed her when she fell under extreme stress. When it struck, she always recognized it. These would be the prime days for a stupid argument. Though she tried to control it, some days it just couldn't be done. She could tell that today would be one of those days. She knew her husband well enough to know that after hearing Rob Maggard's story, he would also be sitting on his last nerve.

From the sofa, Deborah heard her husband close the bathroom door at his usual time. She heard the timer and the coffee dripping. Removing her blanket, she walked back to the bedroom and slid beneath the comforter Dave had spread across the bed. He didn't usually bother her, knowing she'd be attempting to get more rest.

By nine a.m., she was back up, brushing her teeth, still covered by a dark heaviness, tears sitting at the edge of her lids waiting to pour out. It wouldn't take much to explode.

When Deborah entered the kitchen, Dave was sitting at the table reading the morning news from the Internet.

"Good morning," she said in a dry tone. Walking to the counter, she poured coffee into the cup that Dave had set out for her.

"Bad night?" he asked.

"Yeah, I don't think it's going to be a very good day," she said, and sat down in a chair at the table. "If I get any phone calls about the book fund, please take messages. I can already tell I'm just not up to talking to anyone today."

Dave looked at her as always and asked, "What's wrong?"

A storm surge swept from Deborah's eyes and down her face.

"Everything is wrong," she sobbed. "I don't feel like I have anyone to talk to. I'm afraid to talk to you because I'm afraid you'll get upset, mad, walk off, or yell at me because you don't like to talk and you don't like crying. It's always been that way."

"Here we go again," Dave said, sounding aggravated.

"See, I knew it. Let me try to express my feelings and you can't stand it. David, we have to be able to talk to one another. That's what husbands and wives are supposed to be able to do. For all the wonderful things about you that I've always been in love with, how you protect me, provide for me, rub my feet, or make my coffee, you have never been able to give me the most important thing I ever needed. Communication. Discussing problems and dealing with them without a fight. All the years I've known you, when it came to you being stressed with the Marine Corps or Patrick, I saw you as thick and hard as oak. That's good for some things, but not a marriage. It has always separated me from you. I couldn't get across it or through it to understand what you were dealing with or feeling. You have never let me in when we both needed it most."

Dave looked at her with a stern face and shook his head.

"So what is it? What do you want to talk about?" Dave asked.

"I can't stand all the news from the TV that you saturate yourself in. It's not helping. If happiness is going to come to this house again, you've got to start thinking on good things. You've got to ask God's help like I'm trying to do or you're—we're—going to remain miserable. And I can't stand that, and I can't carry this darkness forever. I need for you to talk to me about Patrick. What you're feeling. I need to see you cry and hold onto me so I can comfort you. Until you let me, I don't know what else to do or say. I feel so alone most times because we can't talk. I feel regret because we never had a child of our own."

She couldn't believe she said that. It was an old pain she'd tried to forget.

"I have the same regret," Dave said in a solemn, sincere voice.

Deborah couldn't believe what he'd just said. In her heart and deep from her memory she knew why Dave had told her years ago that they didn't need more children. He had told her once during a heated argument that he hadn't wanted any more because he was afraid of trying to be a father again since he felt he'd failed with Patrick. Because he'd never had a father himself and didn't know how he was supposed to raise a child. And in her heart she knew she'd had her tubal ligation when she was thirty-three to make sure there were no slipups. But subconsciously she had blamed Dave because he had signed the papers, never trying to stop her, and she had hated herself for destroying her ability to have another child. Seeing Patrick all those years as the other woman's son and not her own, when she had invested so much time in him, had always left her feeling shortchanged and full of sadness, especially after Jason had chosen to live with his dad in Georgia. All of it had led to years of resentment that had finally driven her to leave Dave and return to Georgia.

"No one can ever fill your boots," she'd told him often, "even though you've got a mean twin inside you."

Deborah looked closely at Dave's eyes. Tears welled inside them. His lips trembled as he spoke.

"You don't know how much I die every day when I get up. I'll never get another phone call or e-mail from him. I'll never hear, 'Hey Dad, I love you,' again. Do you know how many times I walk into that garage and cry because I regret the times I was so hard on him with the yelling, the time I hit him, or kicked him out of the house. The time I couldn't spend with him when he was little because of the Marine Corps. You just don't know how I wish I could change all that. How much I miss him. How much I want to tell him again that I love him."

Deborah stood from her chair, stepped next to her husband, placed her arms around his shoulders, pulling his head to her stomach as he clung to her and wept.

Regaining her own composure she hugged her husband tightly.

"Honey, you have nothing to regret. Please believe that. You were the best father that you knew how to be, and that was a good one. You can't blame your job. It was your family's livelihood. Patrick never lacked for anything. I didn't know his mother, but you can't help what she did or didn't do in your absence. You had no choice but to discipline him the best way you knew how during those years that he was hanging with the wrong crowd. If you hadn't played tough love he would have never had reason to change his direction. He was already spoiled. Not sending him out when he was older and not wanting to follow house rules would have encouraged him to always have his way. He could have killed himself on heroin instead of dying a hero. Please try and see the bigger picture. Some parents lose to the drugs after they've done everything in their power to make a difference. That doesn't make them bad parents. And it doesn't mean their child was lost.

"I'm not so sure that every human being doesn't choose their time to enter this world, and the time to leave, on the terms meant only for them. Children are lost to car accidents, health problems, or drowning. We all know there's a time we have to leave this earth. And it's worse when it's your child, but these things are not in our hands. We're only the vessels to bring a child into the world. We can't control how they're taken from us. You did the right things, honey. Look at how he turned out. Look at all he accomplished. Look who he wanted to make so proud. Look who he wanted to be like. It was you, honey. He got his sweetness, his strength and determination from you and because of you."

Deborah bent down and placed kisses on her husband's head. She squeezed him again as tight as she could.

Dave looked at his wife. "I love you so much," he said. "I'd never make it without you".

~ NINETEEN ~

IN COVINGTON, LOUISIANA, Kacee walked from the classroom where she had just completed her last week of graduate study, which would allow her to teach kindergarten. This had been the dream that Patrick had encouraged her to pursue. Keeping busy with courses and studying through June and July had been the saving grace that kept her from continually dwelling on Patrick and lost dreams. She also held on to how blessed she was to be home and to be a teacher in the United States.

She would never forget the schoolrooms she visited in Afghanistan. If not bombed to pieces, they were wood shacks with dirt floors. And on the walls, instead of colorful bulletin boards with ABCs, playful animal characters, or flower gardens, there were posters of various land mines and weapons the children were taught to recognize. Many of the Guard units had worked hard to gain school supplies from folks back home while helping rebuild schools for the Afghan children. When she and other soldiers went off base to the local dusty towns, their hearts were torn as the children they saw begged for water or food. And though she had loved the beautiful mountain range she could see from her office at Bagram, she was happy to be home, to be a woman from America who wasn't required to cover her head and face. She knew her experiences had provided the knowledge to realize all the numerous blessings she had to be thankful for, even in the midst of all that had occurred over the past six months. And moments ago, with a call on her cell phone, she received, unexpectedly, another gift she couldn't wait to call and tell her sisters and Deborah about.

In Georgia, Deborah answered the phone. Kacee's first words were, "You won't believe what happened to me today! I've got a teacher's dream job!"

Deborah knew that Kacee had a bittersweet feeling about returning to the school that she'd won Teacher of the Year from before leaving for Afghanistan. It was in a low-income area where parents weren't the most supportive and a lot of children had behavioral problems. The school budget was so low the teachers bought most of their own supplies for bulletin boards or teaching.

"So, what happened? Tell me!"

Deborah looked toward Dave in his corner on the sofa. The rise in his brow told her he was wondering what she was so excited and loud about. She listened while Kacee explained how one of her professors, who was also the principal at a local Episcopalian school, had recommended she go there for an interview. The school had an opening for a kindergarten teacher.

"It just came out of nowhere!" Kacee said. "I couldn't believe that I wasn't looking for anything different, and this dropped right in my lap! I just got the call; they want me for the job!"

Deborah was so happy for Kacee that she was almost in tears.

Kacee shared how great her new environment was going to be and that instead of having to drive forty-five minutes to get to work, it would now take only fifteen at most.

"Well, it looks like Patrick is still looking out for you," Deborah told her.

"I know he is," Kacee said.

"Well, why do you think they were so impressed?"

Deborah listened as Kacee told her about the essay the graduate students had been required to write, telling why they wanted to be kindergarten teachers, and how they could make a difference in a child's life. In her essay she talked about having lost both Patrick and her mother over the past months. She told about her experiences in Afghanistan, how she knew she needed to be with children she could nurture and who could help nurture her. The essay had apparently been the key that provided the serendipitous gift.

"Well, there you go!" Deborah told her. "Good things do come to those who believe. And who deserve. And you've certainly earned every good thing that can come your way, sweetie."

"I want to thank you and Dave for raising a son like Patrick," Kacee said. "He worked so hard to make me believe and have confidence again. And by the way, I'm driving to Georgia this coming weekend. I want to be a part of the party for the book registrations."

Since his love for reading had played a major role in Patrick's life, a memorial fund had been created to provide books on a monthly basis to children under the age of five. The project kept Deborah and Dave busy registering children to receive free books, reading stories in classrooms and at the library, and discovering how generous friends and strangers were to contribute funds in Patrick's memory. Deborah kept a poem on the refrigerator door called "Busy Being Kind." A line in the poem spoke of relieving one's own heartache by taking time to help others.

"I'll drive up on Friday," Kacee said. "I'll call if I get lost. You know I have no sense of direction!"

"We'll be waiting on you," Deborah assured Kacee.

Late Friday evening Kacee arrived safely at the Tainsh home after calling only twice to find her way. She did have one thing on her mind to find out from Deborah, if she could find the nerve to ask. She still felt in the dark about the ghosts that Patrick had told her he needed to tell her about.

Deborah and Dave met her at the door.

"I think you know where your room is," Deborah said.

Kacee walked into the room with the big window facing the backyard, the one with the candles on the table next to the queen-sized bed where she and Patrick had cuddled during that one grand week during Christmas holidays, the one where she had stayed before leaving for Afghanistan and when she returned for Patrick's memorial. The room she knew she would always be able to come to if she needed it. This was her new extended family. Another gift brought her way.

This time she noticed the painting of a bright colorful field of wild flowers on a mountain beneath a pristine blue sky that Deborah had hung on the wall near the bed. It looked like something only heaven could create.

"Are you hungry?" Deborah asked, poking her head inside the bedroom door.

"A little. But I want to take a shower first. I feel grimy."

"Okay, you do that while Dave gets the grill ready. We'll have some steaks and 'taters. Jason and Sindy will be here by then."

Later that night, Deborah and Kacee sat in the rocking chairs on the back porch listening to the mating noise of the cicadas and watching the moths in the yellow fanlight on a hot muggy July night. Dave lit the flambeaus to smoke away the mosquitoes.

"So, I know you're excited about the job, but how are things otherwise?" Deborah asked.

"I'm doing okay, I guess. I go through my crying spells. But I know I just have to keep moving forward. It's hard. But I know that's what Patrick would want me to do. And I know he can't stand all this crying!" Kacee tried to laugh.

"I'm sure," Deborah said. "He's that much like his dad. Can't stand crying women."

"I did want to tell you that a friend I met at school wants me to meet her brother. He's been divorced for about a year and has two children. But I don't know if I'm ready for that, yet."

"Well, sweetie, that's something only you'll know when the time is right. But don't close any doors," Deborah told her. "You don't know when you're making a good friend. And you know that Dave and I want you to meet someone that will make you happy. I know how important it is to you to have children of your own. But don't rush. Take your time. I think we should all know by now that we can't make some things happen. They just have to come or go when they're supposed to."

Deborah took sips from her bottled water.

"I know," Kacee said. "I think it's going to be hard. Patrick was something special. The way he could get me to talk, the way he was so patient with me and all my insecurities."

"Well, listen," Deborah said. "If a great job can drop in your lap out of nowhere, who says a great guy won't, again, at the right time? And so what if he doesn't? Look at all you've got going for you. Honey, if I had accomplished by thirty-three all that you have, nobody could've touched me!" Deborah said with a laugh.

"Yeah, but I still want children of my own," Kacee said.

"I know you do. But if you don't, look at all the beautiful children being placed in your care every day."

Deborah, sitting with her feet on Patrick's footstool and rocking easily, looked at Kacee and smiled.

"I need to tell you about my best girlfriend in the world," Deborah said. "In 1984 when we all lived in Oceanside, I worked for a small bank. A coworker's husband was also in the Marine Corps. He was a recon pilot. He flew OV-10s. Sharon and Scott were only twenty-seven at the time. They had been married for about three years and were the couple everyone envied. They met in college at UCLA and married after graduation. 'Poor as dirt,' Sharon used to tell me. But they were so happy. Sharon always said that they were each other's best friend. They loved to make margaritas, have beach parties, and dance. And Scott loved to surf. He grew up in California. Sharon was from Washington State. I'll never forget the Halloween Sharon and I both dressed up in French maid costumes for work. Afterward we went to a popular place that had good bands and dancing. It wasn't far from where Dave and I lived. Sharon and Scott lived on base. Dave didn't want to join us, so Sharon and I went after work and waited for Scott. He rode his motorcycle from the base, dressed as a grim reaper. I remember being so envious of how he and Sharon laughed and danced, having the time of their lives. I actually won a bottle of champagne that night by sitting on and popping the most balloons that were scattered on the floor."

Deborah took another drink of water while Kacee laughed, trying to imagine the scene.

"I think it was in the spring of 1984 that several OV-10 pilots crashed and died while training at Pendleton. Sharon told me one day that she had told Scott they needed more life insurance, joking of course, because of the plane crashes. She said Scott told her, 'If I go, it'll be on my motorcycle. Not in my plane. Anyway, you don't need more insurance. I'm not going to leave you with a bunch of money that'll bring a bunch of single guys to your front door.'"

Deborah recalled how Sharon had laughed about the conversation. Then she continued.

"I'll never forget the day of July 31, 1985. Our senior loan officer took a call at the bank. We were all close friends, more so than a lot of brothers and sisters. Lee had to carry the message alone for hours after the call came from Camp Pendleton saying Scott had gone down in a flight exercise. He had been instructed to prepare a room where the chaplain could come and meet with Sharon."

Deborah looked at Kacee. "Honey, I'm telling you this story to let you know that I've shared this pain with another dear person. To tell you that if Sharon were here to talk to you, she'd tell you that life will go on and you can make it with perseverance and by never losing hope. To keep on living and enjoying a day at a time the best you can. Sharon and Scott never had children. She lost her soul mate and best friend at twenty-seven. Then when she was thirty-two and still single, her pap smear showed she needed an immediate full hysterectomy because of cancer cells. I was there for that, too. And I'll tell you, I've never been around anyone who showed the strength through all those years of hell like she did. She never let any of her friends see her cry. Although she shared with me that she did most of her crying at night, just like you do. It was probably eight years later that she went through boxes of Scott's belongings and started getting rid of things. I have always felt privileged that I was the one sitting in her living room with her, going through those precious things as she decided what to do with items like his flight suit and OV-10 model. And I can tell you this too, in the years after Scott's death, she kissed a lot of frogs, some that I warned and threatened her about."

Deborah laughed, getting a laugh from Kacee, too.

"Ours is what you can honestly call a true, never faltering friendship. We shared so many good and bad times while we both lived in California. We go for years now without visits, but when we get on the phone, our conversations go on like we live next door to one another."

"So how is she doing now?" Kacee asked.

"She's doing great. After ten years, she finally remarried. And to boot it was someone she and Scott knew at college. He was in their wedding. His name is Dan, and he had never married. He was a nuclear engineer on a navy submarine. After Scott's death, any time he was in San Diego, he'd call Sharon to see how she was doing and take her to dinner. Anyway, to make a long story short, the time came when he told her that he had loved her for quite a while and wanted her to marry him. She was afraid at first that it would ruin their great platonic relationship. But when she called me and we talked, I encouraged her to go for it. And she did. Of course they talked a lot about their expectations in a marriage. Everything from religion to politics. And they're so happy now it'll make you sick! Even in North Dakota where Dan is from."

The two women laughed again.

"So, it can happen again, can't it?" Kacee asked, looking at Deborah.

"Sure it can, if it's meant to be. And I think that's where our faith has to take hold, accepting the path meant for our lives. I know it's not easy. I sure battle with all of it, but, as Einstein said, 'God doesn't play dice.'"

"I know. That's what I've got to believe, too," Kacee said, rocking back and forth in the cane back rocker, thinking how she could possibly ask Deborah about Patrick's ghosts.

"Hey, aren't you gals ready to come in yet? I bet the mosquitoes are having a ball with you," Dave said, walking to the side of the porch to smoke a cigarette.

"Nah, we're doing fine." Kacee told him.

"Well, it's eleven o'clock. I'm going to bed. We have to get up early. You two better get some sleep."

"We know, we know," Deborah said to her husband as he bent down to give her a kiss, then walked over with a hug for Kacee. "Alright then, I'll see you two later. Good night."

"Good night to you, too."

After Dave left, Kacee asked Deborah how he was doing these days.

"Better, much better, I think. We had a good cry and a good talk the other day. It was one of my small miracles. Or maybe I should say, great big miracles. He finally told me about the anger he felt at himself for times he felt he'd treated Patrick wrong years ago. And the time he missed spending with him when he was little because of the military life. I did my best to convince him he'd done nothing that he needed to carry guilt for. It's because of him that Patrick finally turned a corner and became the man that he did."

Kacee finally felt it time to ask the question she needed the answer to.

"I have something I need to ask you about. And I'm hoping it won't upset you. When Patrick and I were e-mailing each other between Iraq and Afghanistan, there was a time he mentioned having some ghosts that he needed to tell me about. He had said he'd tell me when we were home. Do you know what he meant by that?"

Deborah sighed, watching the fire at the end of the flambeaus burning at the porch corners. This was a subject she had wondered if Patrick would ever find a way to tell Kacee about. She had even mentioned it to Dave before the two of them deployed. She had not felt it right for Patrick to hide his past drug habit from Kacee if he truly loved her and wanted to marry her. But it had not been her place to interfere with his or Kacee's life. She had known that Kacee was the caliber of woman that Patrick wanted and needed in his new life and who was so welcomed in their family. She feared, probably as Patrick had, how Kacee would react if she knew. Now, it was her responsibility to tell Kacee, since Patrick had apparently opened the door and wanted her to know the truth.

"Yes, I think I know what he was referring to," Deborah said softly, watching Kacee's expression. "First let me ask you this. Do you remember when you told me that you and Patrick told me and Dave that you met at a Wal-Mart because you were afraid we'd think you were weird or nuts if we knew he met you through the Internet? But after you built enough trust with us, you told me the truth."

"Yes, I remember."

"Well, with what I'm about to tell you, just keep in mind that Patrick needed to gain your trust, he knew you weren't the kind of woman who would've wanted the man he once was. But the man he became was one any woman should have been proud to call hers. Patrick was always very smart, book smart because he read a lot and street smart because he knew that side of life, too. Before joining the Army, he lived a rough life for reasons that God only knows. As his friend, Chris, once told me, Patrick was a wild pony who wasn't going to be tamed until he was ready. And until then, he lived life rebelliously and the way he wanted, like it or not."

Deborah went on to add to what she had already shared with Kacee weeks ago about the Tainsh family life in California. She recalled to Kacee the wild, carefree life that Patrick had been allowed to live in Virginia Beach when his dad was away and how some people close to him fooled with marijuana and no telling what else. How he rebelled in California, but never got caught at home with marijuana or cigarettes. Then Deborah went on to tell what she felt finally caused Patrick to cross the line to heroin that almost cost him his life.

"I've thought a lot about what went on with Patrick. He was running wild and in bad company during one of the most critical years of his life. He was twelve when his dad was in Japan for a year. On top of that, during the same time, his mom dumped his dad to marry a guy who couldn't deal with Patrick's behavior. Then he had to move to California, away from everything and everyone he knew. Then he had a new stepmom to deal with who had rules. A few years later his mother died. I think that by then he felt lost with no hope, consumed with internal anger." Deborah continued speaking as Kacee listened without saying a word.

"When Dave brought him back to California after his mother's memorial, I gave him a card and a very long letter I wrote in an attempt to give him hope. I told him his mother was with God, a part of God, and that life on earth wasn't the final destination. I wrote out some simple Bible quotes for him. It was all I knew to do. I knew he was in pain, but like his dad, he didn't know how to talk about it or deal with it at the time. I gave him hugs and comforted him as best I could. He was seventeen. Then sometime after his eighteenth birthday, he decided he didn't want to live in our house anymore. He didn't want to finish school and take on the responsibilities required if he was going to live there for free. I believe that after he moved out, he fell in with the bad company including some freaky band group that he got caught up in and went south, so to speak."

Deborah told Kacee, in the best way she could, everything about Patrick's most difficult times in life. How she and Dave constantly begged him and offered him the help he needed to straighten out his life. About the time his dad picked him up from the alley and took him to rehab and all that had occurred over the years to the time of his decision to join the Army. How once there, he had become the best that anyone could ask for.

"All this is why I've said he was a walking miracle." Deborah smiled and took another drink of water. She and Kacee sat quietly for a few moments.

"That's incredible," Kacee finally said. "God, he came so far. No wonder he kept encouraging me. Being patient and not giving up when I kept running from him. He knew what it was like to be in pain and still have others out there waiting to provide help when he was ready. The way he was all makes sense now. I thought he was too good to be true, but he was just being there for me like others were for him. Hearing all this just makes me love him more."

Both women wiped tears from their faces, then stood to hug each other as a soft breeze rustled the wind chimes above their heads and a hawk sat silent on the oak limb.

~ TWENTY ~

DEBORAH WAS MORE THAN pleased with the children's story time and book party on Saturday morning at the city's recreation center. Friends and family worked as volunteers to provide stories and puppet shows for the kids and parents. Twenty children were registered to receive a free book every month for a year thanks to Patrick's memorial fund. More children would be registered on another day. When a news reporter showed up and interviewed Kacee, she said it so well: "Patrick was my hero, now he's a hero for these children."

"Well, that was great," Dave said as he loaded Deborah's homemade puppet box into his truck. "Everyone seemed to have a good time."

"And the weather cooperated. It looks like it's going to be a great day," Jason said, hugging his mom and congratulating her for the work she'd done. "I think Sindy and I'll head on home. See you guys later."

Jason hugged Dave, then walked toward Sindy and Kacee to interrupt their conversation.

Deborah gave her husband a kiss. "Well, honey, Kacee and I'll meet you at home. I need to stop by the mall on the way. Thanks for all your help. Couldn't have done it without you."

Back at the house, Dave pressed the button on the answering machine to listen to messages. There was one message—the one he most wanted to hear.

"Sergeant Major, this is Colonel Padrone at Fort Polk. I wanted to let you know that we have received your son's Silver Star. I'd like to speak with you about a ceremony for presentation to you and your family."

This had been the last missing piece to closure, and it still weighed on Dave's mind. He had made call after call and written his congressman to find out what the delay was. He wanted to make sure that nothing belonging to Patrick got lost in the bureaucracy and business of the war.

Dave dialed the number left by the colonel, who had been kind enough to call from home. After a discussion and looking at the calendar a date was set. He and Deborah would go to Fort Polk for the formal ceremony, which would be the last military honor that his son would receive.

Two weeks later on a Wednesday morning at a quarter to nine, under a crystal blue sky and bearable August temperature, Dave, Deborah, and Kacee were escorted as VIPs to Dragoon Field at Fort Polk, Louisiana. Deborah noticed that the groomed green field sat next to regimental headquarters and the museum where Patrick had escorted Dave and her over two years ago, explaining the history of his beloved Second Armored Cavalry Regiment. At the end of the museum building sat Dragoon Park, existing to honor ACR troopers. Retired helicopters, tanks like those once used by Hussein's Republican Guard, and an Iraqi anti-aircraft gun still used by third world countries were placed one next to the other. From days of the iron curtain sat a piece of the gray, concrete wall and markers that once separated East from West Germany. Before the wall came down, the Second Armored Cavalry Regiment maintained surveillance covering 731 kilometers from 1947 to March 1, 1990.

Dave and Deborah had been told earlier that the regiment was being relocated from Fort Polk to Fort Lewis, Washington, probably by the end of November. When they asked about the museum, they learned that all of it would shift with the name of the unit. Many of the soldiers who had been a part of this historical group as scouts and defenders were being reassigned to different areas outside their beloved cavalry. Deborah thought it ironic that they were closing a door to Patrick's military life and the unit he had loved and found his perfect place with.

The van stopped in front of the reviewing stand covered by a yellow and white tent. They would sit there with officers and officials attending the ceremony. Five formations of cavalry troops in their green camouflage—Regimental, Eagle, Ghost, Howitzer, and Engineers—stood on the field. Patrick had been a part of Eagle troop. "Apropos," Deborah thought with a smile in her heart. Native Americans believed the eagle a representation of leadership, regarded as the eyes of the Creator because it flies so high and close to the Great Spirit. They also believed the eagle's feathers helped to gather and maintain courage for a fearless drive, to perform worthwhile deeds under extreme conditions. Patrick had certainly left this world doing just that.

Dave, Deborah, and Kacee took their places as a greeting line formed with generals, colonels, captains, lieutenants, base protocol, the mayor of Leesville, and a gentleman from the Department of the Army who shook their hands and gave thankful condolences. Officers' wives extended kind remarks and hugs. And most special, standing next to Dave, was Patrick's commanding officer, whose presence Dave had requested. Captain Corn had been with Patrick during his last moments in Baghdad.

From behind her sunglasses, Deborah surveyed the field and the soldiers who stood there, young men and women, some friends of Patrick's, who were now a new era of veterans and would probably soon rotate again to continue the battle in the War on Terrorism. The regiment had lost at least seven men over the past year in Iraq. How many more of them would give their lives to keep America free from attacks like the one of September 11th? At the far corner of the field to her left, next to Dragoon Park, Deborah stared at the lone soldier, who in cavalry tradition wore the cavalry Stetson with a gold band and acorns, the dark blue shirt, and light blue trousers. Deborah had learned that the light blue trousers came from the early years of cavalrymen when their dark blue ones were hung on their saddles and faded from the sun. With knee-high boots over his pant legs, the soldier stood like a statue from the past, holding the reins of a chestnut quarter horse, saddled with no rider, and empty boots turned backward in the stirrups.

At nine a.m., everyone stood for the invocation followed by the national anthem. The regimental commander followed with the remarks about why Patrick had been posthumously awarded the Silver Star for gallantry in action against an enemy of the United States while engaged in military operations:

> For exceptionally valorous achievement as a gunner on the night of 11 February, 2004. During an enemy ambush involving an Improvised Explosive Device (IED), Sergeant Tainsh, in complete disregard for his own safety and well being, returned fire while mortally wounded, allowing aid to be rendered to his fellow soldiers. His professionalism, leadership, and courage under fire, and performance of duty against such overwhelming odds uphold the finest traditions of military service and reflects great credit upon him, the 2nd Armored Cavalry Regiment, Combined Joint Task Force Seven, and the United States Army.

Standing between her husband and Kacee, Deborah hid her tears behind the sunglasses. With her left hand she held Dave's hand, then placed her right arm around Kacee's shoulders, pulling her close. When the remarks concluded, Dave walked to the field to be presented with the Silver Star on behalf of his son. Tears streamed down Deborah's and Kacee's faces as they watched him stand at attention, stoic and proud, in coat and tie as the presentation was made and the framed gold medal with the Silver Star in the center was placed in his hands.

Following the closing prayer and another wave of heart-felt thank yous and condolences, men who had served with Patrick stood in line to share words and stories about their fallen comrade. Deborah knew that she and Dave could stand all day and listen to soldier after soldier share stories about Patrick's life from the past year.

"Sergeant Major, I'm Lieutenant Willson. I'll always remember Patrick for giving me the nickname, 'Big Head,' from the movie

Jerry Maguire. He kept us going, sir. We'll miss him." Smiles broke across everyone's face.

"We shared a lot of time sleeping together on the Humvee," said another lieutenant, who had served six months with Patrick when they first entered Iraq. "I'd sleep on the hood and Sergeant Tainsh would be on the roof next to his fifty caliber. The funniest time I remember was when we were all so tired and running with no sleep for about twenty hours. We were in convoy headed for Najaf. We'd kick and punch one another to make sure we stayed awake. When we finally got to a spot where we could get some rest, I fell asleep on the hood, and Pat was on the roof. I woke up when I heard a loud thump, thump, and then moaning. I thought we had been ambushed. When I jumped off the hood to see what was happening, I saw Sergeant Tainsh on the ground next to the vehicle. He had turned in his sleep and rolled off the top of the Humvee and hit the open door on his way down, crashing on the ground. We laughed the rest of the night about it. He was always a good sport about anything and he was a damn good soldier. He always made sure I had everything I needed to run the platoon."

Stories passed from the troops for about an hour that morning, all of them providing the best memories about patience, friendship, humor, leadership, and courage that Patrick Tainsh had left behind for his family, friends, and comrades. Dave, Deborah, and Kacee thought that they had heard it all, until a staff sergeant spoke. He told them that Patrick's memory would live on as a training tool for other soldiers.

"It's not the Silver Star that will mean anything to the troops," he said. "It'll be knowing about the man behind it. Tainsh was the greatest example of what a soldier should be. I don't remember him ever, not one time, complaining about a single thing the entire time we were over there. He always had a smile and something positive or funny to say. And he never, ever, showed a single sign of fear. Some of us would actually get mad because we couldn't figure out how he could do it, how he could always remain so calm and focused, always ready to do the job. I know I would dread going out on another patrol. I'd sit and complain, but not Tainsh. He'd just say 'Let's go. Let's get it done.' And then mount up on his Humvee like it was just another day at the park. Then he always wanted to talk about how to make the patrols better. He always reached for the next level. Just two nights before he died, we were ambushed. But he never even acted like it happened. He was amazing."

Deborah stood next to Dave, squeezing his hand. She looked up at him, then at the troops with a smile and said, "He was just like his dad." Then she wondered if Patrick had ever told his buddies about the No Fear surf shirts that he once wore and the tattoo for strength that was on his wrist.

After thanking the troops, Deborah and Dave hugged Kacee goodbye. She was headed back home to Covington while Deborah and Dave left for Georgia. The sun reflected off blue sky as Deborah interlocked her fingers with Dave's. An oldies station played tunes from the '70s and '80s. Riding across Interstate 10 and passing by the New Orleans skyline, Dave turned up the volume. Harry Chapin's voice floated from the speakers with "Cat's in the Cradle."

"Me and Patrick used to talk about that song," Dave said, focusing on the highway in front of him.

"What did you talk about?" Deborah asked, looking at her husband's profile while gently stroking the side of his face with her fingers.

"How we both always had good intentions of spending more time with one another. But it just didn't happen like we wanted it to."

"Well, I thought everything was wonderful today, but emotionally draining. How are you feeling, sweetie?"

Dave took a moment before answering, then looking forward, he responded to his wife. "Proud and humbled," he said, "proud and humbled."

~ TWENTY-ONE ~

A WEEK FOLLOWING THE CEREMONY, Dave looked into his wife's face. "Do you love me?"

"Of course I do, you silly!" Deborah looked up to her husband from her cozy place beneath the white comforter. He was standing beside the bed with his hands in his jeans pockets, a melancholy look on his face that she had learned to read, even if he did not always confess what was going on behind it. They had both been up at two-thirty this morning. It was not unusual for her to be rambling around the house and turning the television on at that time of night. But when they were both up and watching an old Danny Kay movie together, she knew something had to be bothering him. All he told her was that he couldn't sleep. But she had seen that forlorn look in his face, and instead of pressing him she just hugged him, thinking that he must have awakened from a disturbing dream. By five-thirty, they returned to bed, but Dave had risen by seven and left her to sleep until almost noon.

"Is something wrong?"

Dave grinned. "No, nothing's wrong. I just needed to hear you say it again."

"I love you, I love you, I love you!"

"I'm so glad." Dave bent down and kissed his wife on the forehead. "When you get up, there's an e-mail I think you'll enjoy reading. It's from an Iraqi interpreter in Baghdad who spent time with Patrick."

"You're kidding?"

"Nope. And you won't believe what time it came in. While we were up at two-thirty, the e-mail came from Iraq. You know why I was up?"

"I was hoping you'd tell me." Deborah said, knowing her intuition had been right.

"I was dreaming about Patrick, about when I went to his graduation after boot camp. After the dinner that night and we went to the hotel, he asked me to go back downstairs and have a beer with him. I was so tired, I told him I just couldn't. I woke up this morning regretting I didn't do that."

Deborah removed the covers and stood in front of her husband, placing her arms around him. "I knew you had been dreaming. I know that look you get on your face and in your eyes. Honey, these are the things you have to tell me about or I worry about you. As far as feeling regret, Patrick understood and still does."

Deborah was glad to see Dave pull out a smile and laugh in a way that could light up a room.

"I'll never forget how Patrick laughed that night at the graduation dinner. The captain had the newbies doing crazy exercises, moving their hands and arms in all kinds of crazy motions. Instead of being embarrassed, Patrick laughed his butt off."

Deborah smiled, envisioning Patrick's face as Dave spoke. For the first time, he was telling her about one of his dreams. He talked about Patrick on his own. She felt her heart was sitting on wings.

"Come read that message," he said. "You'll love it."

Deborah followed her husband to the kitchen where the laptop sat on the table.

The message was in broken English.

Dear sirs:

First of all, I'm sending this e-mail to say sorry for your great family about losing your son, may be it's too late to say that, because I have no address of e-mail to say that. I'm very grateful to Captain Corn who gave me your e-mail to make my contacts, already I was thinking how to make my contacts with you to say sorry and to tell you how late Tainsh was. He was very great man, hero, I never saw him afraid, he was like eagle, even Captain described him the eye of the Eagle troops. Late Tainsh was like a brother to me and to other soldiers, he was always taking care of me, because I was the only civilian among them (the interpreter). My name is Ahmed from Iraq, Baghdad, I would like to be your friend as I was a friend to Tainsh, once, he told me I wish to visit us in the U. S., and I let you meet my family there. I worked with him almost ten months, I will not forget him, never, always looking with our pictures taken together, here, in Baghdad with other soldiers, he was with us, I ask God to grant you more and more patience for losing this great guy. Excuse me for my language, just I'm not native speaker.

Yours,

The interpreter of Eagle troops

With her hand, Deborah wiped tears from the side of her face.

"That's wonderful. See, just when a bad feeling comes along, we get a wonderful message. Patrick is still looking after you." She looked up at Dave standing beside her, his hands on her shoulders.

"I'll return Ahmed's message," she said. "I'll let him know how much we appreciate his words and that Patrick's invitation always stands." Then she wondered if Ahmed knew that in America the eagle stands for courage.

~ TWENTY-TWO ~

LIKE A GOSSAMER SCARF, the morning sun floated through the dining room windows. Motes, tiny angels, danced inside the light drifting across the table, beyond the dining room entry, and against Deborah's curio hanging on the wall in the hallway. The collection of miniature Swarovski crystals, in various shapes that included a butterfly, squirrel, and the deer that Patrick had instructed his dad to buy for Deborah last Christmas, reflected every color of the rainbow. With help from his dad, Patrick had begun the collection for her the Christmas he was fourteen.

On her way down the hall, the light and rainbows reflecting off the cream colored wallpaper attracted Deborah's attention. She stopped as she often did to silently thank Patrick and examine the clarity and beauty of the crystal menagerie. How colors of the rainbow sparkled in each one and bounced off the walls. She remembered an analogy that she had read from a book on the Kabbalah. It essentially said that all are vessels made from the same hands, with the same light emanating through all. But the reflection in which that light appears depends on what the vessel contains. Put different colored water inside clear vessels and let sunlight fall through each one, and you'll get a different color from each. She smiled, thinking about the various colors that emanated from her family, both of blood and beyond, and from the entire world: sinners, saints, terrorists, and heroes, just everyday people of every faith. All different vessels made from the same hands with the same light flowing through, but with circumstances and environments that created the various colors of light that ultimately reflected in what seemed a confused world, if one forgot their source.

After coffee and Dave's favorite Sunday breakfast of bacon and pancakes, Deborah sat in her rocker on the deck, her feet propped on Patrick's stool. With full sun, the day was an exception to the normal August temperatures. A light breeze flowed through the tall trees with a sound like gentle surf washing against shore, a sound that always reminded her of Patrick.

Deborah watched her husband. He seemed to be doing better. The day before, he had received an extra boost when mail arrived from Patrick's friend, Bob Blankenship, who was at Fort Knox. When Dave handed her the envelope, Deborah pulled out a birth announcement. There was a sonogram picture and the words:

Have You Heard?
Bob and Laura Blankenship
are having a new baby boy
Patrick Shannon Blankenship
Due January 2005

"What an honor," Dave had said as they both wiped tears from their eyes.

This morning, Dave was scrubbing the deck furniture with diluted Clorox while smoke swirled above his head. He liked to have things in perfect order when company was coming. He always cleaned and groomed everything like when he was on active duty preparing for a general's inspection. Today and for the next two days he was setting everything in perfect order for the arrival of some of his former troops from 11th Marines. He had been their first sergeant from the early- to mid-80s when they were stationed at Camp Pendleton; he had trained with the young men for seven months in Okinawa and the Philippines in 1986.

A couple of months before losing Patrick, Dave had answered the phone and a voice had asked, "Is this the home of First Sergeant Tainsh?"

Dave responded, "Well it's the home of now retired Sergeant Major Tainsh."

The young man went on to say, "Well Sergeant Major, this Casey Sexton. I was one of your troops with Delta 2/11." Then he informed Dave that he'd been trying to track him down for a while. He had wanted to let his old first sergeant know how much he appreciated all he did for him when he was a young Marine.

Dave was both flabbergasted and honored. Never had he given thought about leaving any kind of life-affirming impressions on any of his young Marines from those years now gone. After the call, and following news of Patrick's death, a group of the former troops planned to visit for a reunion. Deborah felt it was one of the best things that could happen for her husband. She knew it would take time that couldn't be measured for Dave's and her pain to begin to fade, and she knew it would never totally disappear. But this would be a welcome visit from a group of surrogate sons who were fated to bring good memories and laughter to their home.

Taking a drink of water from the Zephyr Hills bottle, Deborah looked at the tan leather journal that lay in her lap. No entries had been made for months. Today, she finally felt fresh and inspired again. She thought about what she should make note of. What would be of value fifty years from now when some curious person may find the contents of letters, cards, awards, and newspaper articles left inside a brown, world map trunk that would be moved someday from the end of Dave's and her bed and placed in a dusty attic?

Thoughts came to mind to begin a story of her family's journey over the past years. How through all the pain, if one looks, there is much to be learned and gained, with friends and strangers to rely on. How pride flowed through her and Dave with tears, when the Iraqi Olympians and Americans received overwhelming applause as they entered the arena on opening night of the 2004 Summer Olympics. How the Iraqi Olympians no longer had to fear returning home to be tortured if they lost. How with a lot of work, children in Iraq and Afghanistan have a chance for a better future. All this because Patrick and others like him had made the greatest sacrifices to liberate, fight terrorism, and make Americans safer. How hope is that one thing that can never be extinguished as long as the human spirit and faith prevail. How, "to whom much is given, much is asked in return." How America, the greatest nation on earth, had sacrificed many sons and daughters for over two hundred years in the name of freedom. How her family had become an integral part of those sacrifices in the first wars of the twenty-first century. Deborah thought about Patrick's thirty-fourth birthday, which would arrive in just a few days, and how she would like to honor him. With that thought, she opened the journal and began to write. At that moment the red-tail hawk, the prophetic bird with healing powers, soared from the sky and landed in the oak, not fifty feet away.

~ EPILOGUE ~

ELEVEN MONTHS AFTER Patrick's death, on January 30, 2005, Dave and Deborah watched news past midnight as Iraqi people walked as far as thirteen miles to reach voting polls for the first time in fifty years. After ten hours, at least seventy percent of the Iraqi people, including women, had cast their votes. A week earlier, Dave and Deborah had received by mail from Fort Polk, Louisiana, a package containing the notebook Patrick had used in Iraq to write notations from daily briefings. Inside, with no date, he had left his last letter for home.

Hi,

Im writing you this letter BECAUSE SomeThing WENT wrong. It may or may not HAVE BEEN my fault But it was time. I Just WANt you to KNow I trieD to Do the right thing. I CAME HERE to HElp Some people out wHo couldn't Help the situation that they WERE SUBJECT TO. MAYBE SomeDAY THEy will BE ABle TO ENJoy FreeDom As WE Do. As far As me it was a Honor to BE ABle to EXPERIENCE that FREEDom. IT WAS A Honor to fight AND DiE with A AMERICAN FlAG on my sHoulDER. HONOR, thATS A BiG WORD AND SomE PEople DONT KNow wHAt it MEANS, its not something

that HAPPENS right AWAY, its
Something that Builds up inside your
soul. I just want you to know that
IvE Always looked up to you. As
A MAN IvE Always WANTED to BE
Like you AND BE successful.

It may Have not HAPPENED on
your time line like you would've
liked, But I WANTED CERTAIN things
then, IVE MADE some BAD
CHoices in my life ; But I DONT
regret it 1 Bit. sometimes people
HAVE to learn from the mistakes
they MAKE. THAts part of life.
learning right from wrong either
the Hard way or EASY way. I just
Also want you to know that IVE
Always loved you AND Appreciate
the things you'VE DONE or tried
to DO for ME. Sometimes it
WAS HArd to SAY thanks But
I WAS Always thankful FoR you.
I Also want to say Im SORRY
FoR All the Hurt IVE DONE
in the past. Somethings that
HAPPENED WAS ME But it WASNY
ME. I HOPE you Accept my
Apology. SORRY. Just REMEMBER
ME FoR wHo I USED to BE AND
FoR WHO I AM KNOWN AS NOW.
SOMEONE WHO WAS GivIN AN
iNCH But took 10 miles, SOMEONE
wHo LivED life to its fullest AND

wHo DiDNt feAR the coNseQUeNce
of DANGER. SomeoNe wHo LiVED
through touGH times oNly BeCAUSE
HE wANteD them that way, But
turN His life AroUND BeCAUSE HE
wANteD A DiffereNt DEfiNitioN of
fuN iN His life, his JOB AS A
US CAvalry scout. SomeoNe who
loVED surfiNG, music, womEN, His
fAmily. AND his fATHER.
uNtil wE mEET AGAIN, my
HEArt, soul AND love ARE with
you, DoNt EVER forGet that.

LoVE Your soN
PAttick.

One year after Patrick's death, Deborah and Dave discovered the Tragedy Assistance Program for Survivors, a nonprofit organization providing support for anyone grieving the loss of a loved one who has died while serving in the U.S. Armed Forces. In 2005, they attended the TAPS National Military Survivor Seminar, held each Memorial Day weekend in Washington, D.C. There, among more than three hundred survivors, were other parents, spouses, friends, and children, who attended their own Good Grief Camp for Kids. Many were there for the first time; others had returned from past years to provide support to those who followed.

For the first time since Patrick's death, Dave was able to share his feelings with someone other than Deborah. During a break in the seminar, he found himself with another father, speaking about their sons and how they were handling their anger and grief. Later, when Dave, at first reluctant, attended an hour-long TAPS parents' support group, he left commenting, "That should have been two hours instead of one. We all had so much to say."

With Dave's newfound ability to share his grief, Deborah felt as if a boulder had been rolled from her shoulders. That weekend, Deborah, too, talked with many people and received as many hugs as she could give.

Through TAPS, Dave and Deborah were reminded that grief does not end in three days or thirty years. But even with the pain, families can remember together the honorable lives their loved ones led as members of the U.S. Armed Forces and encourage each other as they pick up the pieces. TAPS has taught the Tainshes to "remember the love, celebrate the life, and share the journey." Dave and Deborah became TAPS mentors and continue to speak with other survivors across the nation.

Patrick's legacy lives on in the progress toward freedom in Iraq, in The Sergeant Patrick Tainsh Memorial Books for Children Fund, which has provided more than 8,000 books to more than 400 families, and in Dave and Deborah's continuing work as TAPS mentors.

Donations in memory of Sergeant Patrick Tainsh can be made to TAPS:

Tragedy Assistance Program for Survivors
1621 Connecticut Avenue, NW, Suite 300
Washington, DC 20009

~ OUTSIDE THE WINDOWS ~

We watch out the windows, your dad and I,
wanting to see your easy walk toward
the house to wrap your hand around the brass knob.
Instead we see the chaplain's footprints
we have not been able to scrub from the concrete
and his knuckle prints branded against the door.

Any moment now we will break
through the matrix, reach you,
and pull you back into the kitchen
where you'll show us the proper way to prepare the scallops.

You chose to trade-in your surf board and snowboard
for what you said was something
that would make a difference.

The last time you spoke with your brother
you said, "Don't thank me, it's my job."
You always told your dad and me, "Don't worry."

You climbed in rank faster than most
to reach sergeant; led and taught those
drawn to you like apostles.

On top of the TV we keep the photo of you in
helmet and flak jacket with Iraqi children.
You believed them worth the fight.
You mourned their poverty.

Once defiant, later than most, you followed
steps of your father now accepting with
bitter-sweet pride your folded flag,
cavalry Stetson, silver saber, and bootless spurs.

The Purple Heart, Bronze and Silver Stars carry
the message we want the world to know about You.

We have been reminded, your dad and I, that
God's son began his service at age thirty and at thirty-three
sacrificed himself for human kind.
What coincidence...

In our search we know you dwell in sixty-foot
waves from the North Shore to Australia,
the rain and breeze against the lighthouse chimes.
And outside the family room on a branch of the great oak
you dwell in the noble
heart of the hawk
watching through the window our gradual steps
moving beyond the chaplain's footprints, his knuckle prints
branded against the door.

—We love you always,
   Deb & Dad

~ ACKNOWLEDGMENTS ~

For a duty that goes unacknowledged and an experience they'd rather never know, I want to especially remember with greatest respect two people whose names I'm sure I was told, but would never ask for again until two years after Patrick's death. On behalf of the United States Army, the casualty notification officer and chaplain from Fort Benning, Georgia, had the incomprehensible task of delivering the news of Patrick's death to my husband and me. They represented with grace, professionalism, and compassion those who have come before and will continue to follow when an active duty military person dies. May the military men and women who accept this task always be remembered with the greatest of respect, along with the casualty assistance officers who ensure a family receives all the information and help needed to lay their loved one to rest. Such individuals brought honor to Patrick, our family, themselves, and the United States military. Thank you.

A writer cannot advance a manuscript from its first draft through revisions and edits without a support team. First and foremost, I owe much gratitude to my husband, David, for his patience as I spent hours day and night immersed in writing and rewriting. Thank you for your unconditional love and belief in sharing our and Patrick's story with others. My greatest joy came when you read the words and allowed them to bring us closer together in our darkest days. I'm sure that's what Patrick wanted.

To Amy Childs, Shelly Hall, Jacquelyn Cook, Delane Chappell, Ron Self, Deuce Douglass, Bob Gross, Bridgett Siter, Sherri Neve, Jean Copland, Patty Chamberlain, Harry Franklin, and my writing workshop friends at the Carson McCullers Center for Writers and Musicians in Columbus, Georgia: thank you for your friendship, support, and the time you took to read either parts of or the entire manuscript (some of you more than once) and providing direction, suggestions, edits, and most of all for believing that *Heart of a Hawk* carries a message worth telling, especially in these current days.

And a special thank you to Christy Lyon, my final editor at Elva Resa Publishing. You've the voice of an angel.

~ ABOUT THE AUTHOR ~

DEBORAH TAINSH'S STEPSON, U. S. Army Sergeant Patrick Tainsh, was killed by a roadside bomb in Iraq on February 11, 2004. Writing initially to sort out her own grief, Deborah captured the raw and tender moments of her family's sorrow and remembrance. Her book *Heart of a Hawk: One family's sacrifice and journey toward healing* brings readers into the Tainsh family's living room as Deborah and her husband, retired USMC Sergeant Major David L. Tainsh, hear the tragic news of their son's death and begin their struggle toward acceptance and peace.

A portion of all proceeds from *Heart of a Hawk* is donated to the Tragedy Assistance Program for Survivors, a nonprofit organization offering hope, healing, comfort, and care to thousands of American Armed Forces families facing the death of a loved one each year. As a TAPS mentor, Deborah talks with military families across the nation, sharing her family's continuing journey while celebrating a son's courageous life with the message that "our children expect no less courage and giving from us than what they showed the world." Deborah also promotes early childhood literacy through The Sergeant Patrick Tainsh Memorial Books for Children Fund.

Heart of a Hawk received the Spirit of Freedom Award from Military Writers Society of America. Deborah's poems are included in the National Endowment for the Arts archives of *Operation Homecoming: Writing the Wartime Experience*. She has written for several publications, including *TAPS* magazine, *Marines' Memorial Crossroads Magazine*, and Military.com.

Deborah and David live in the serene woodlands of Harris County, Georgia, near Fort Benning and their son Phillip Jason.